MW01616358

The think tank #NEWDEAL,
dedicated to the positive
transformation of the economy,
is glad to support this book.
More information: newdealhavas.com

Author: Isabelle Grosmaitre
Editing: Cecilia Lim, Leane Jupet, Roxanna Kazemzadeh
Design: Annie Skovgaard Christiansen
Photographer of Author's portrait: Sébastien Cacitti
ISBN 978-2-9596069-0-8

Business
as a Force for
good

How courageous leaders
shift purpose into practice

Isabelle Grosmaitre

To Aurore, Constance, and Paul,

To this new generation of courageous leaders, who act every
day to create a better world — a world
in which economic performance
cannot happen without social progress.

The future is in your hands.

CONTENTS

FOREWORD BY
PAUL POLMAN

The first time I met Isabelle, it was in 2017 in the boardroom of the Consumer Goods Forum in New York. At that time, not many CEOs were ready to embrace the environmental and social challenges at the heart of their model.

After experiencing the hottest week ever recorded last summer, we are now more conscious than ever that we cannot possibly keep going the way we have been. Our world is contending with inequalities, the *climate emergency*[*1], biodiversity loss and geopolitical tensions. We need a system shift. And we have the model: the Sustainable Development Goals. These goals offer an enormous opportunity. We also have the technology: 70% of our issues can be addressed by tech. Besides, the economic facts speak for themselves. **Not acting will cost us more than acting.** If we don't act on climate change, it could cost 178 trillion dollars by 2050. If we take action to reduce global warming by 1.5 degrees, the global economy could gain 43 trillion dollars.

A broad movement in the right direction has begun. The train has left the station. Before COVID, 20% of countries had net zero commitments, while that number is now at 63%. Civil society is speaking up – especially the younger generations, who want companies to have purpose. Companies are accelerating in that direction. Companies that are committed to cut emissions in line with climate science-based targets now represent a third of the global economy. Those that tackle issues of climate change, social cohesion in supply chain and inequalities receive higher valuations from markets. Nonmaterial items are becoming material and valued by markets. Investments are moving in the right direction. Nevertheless, our actions remain too slow. We know what challenges we're facing. The question is how to move at the speed and scale that they require.

We need to move towards a net positive economy, where courageous companies thrive by giving more than they take. *Corporate Social Responsibility** (CSR) is now part of most companies' vocabulary, as they strive to do better by, for instance, reducing plastic production or carbon emissions. But better is not good enough anymore. It is about being sustainable. It is about being regenerative, moving from incremental to transformative. It is about being net positive. We need to ask ourselves how we can put our profits in the service of the problems facing the world. We need to take responsibility. The truth is that this fight we are in for humanity's and the planet's survival is not going to get any easier.

There is a need for partnership towards positive change. How can competitors partner together with civil society and governments to drive transformative change which no single company could deliver alone? Building bridges can be exhausting. Partnership, especially with those you don't always agree with, requires more courage than any act of going-it-alone. And it will likely attract criticism. But it is what the world needs, and we have no other choice.

The challenge standing in the way of making it happens lies not in the science, the money, or the technology. **The biggest challenge is leadership**. People are realizing that things are happening and that the primacy of shareholders which has crept in over the last forty years cannot continue. Shareholders must understand that they need to be led towards a "net positive" mindset. All companies optimize their performance within the parameters of the current system. And this system no longer works. In many boardrooms, there are individuals in positions of power who have succeeded in other fields. Many of them do not have any CSR-related skills. We are not facing a crisis of climate change, inequalities, or food security, but a crisis of apathy, greed, and selfishness. We are facing a crisis of leadership. Getting the right leaders in charge matters.

To the leaders who are eager to drive positive change, who are willing to put a sense of purpose at the heart of their business model, leadership and courage are the crucial piece. Courage comes from the Latin "cor", meaning heart. You are being given the opportunity of a lifetime. Your leadership is needed more than ever.

We are citizens of planet Earth. So, let's act towards a more hopeful future for it.

AUTHOR'S
PRELUDE

I remember the moment I realized that something was at play, a powerful change though I could only make out the early signs. Rather than a single day, I trace it back to an entire year — 2019, the year of the first youth climate march while the northern face of the Olan Mountain, in the Massif des *Écrins*, was collapsing. As a mountain lover, I had spent childhood summers there hiking by lakes, camping, and bathing in icy torrents. That year, both the Alps and the Tibetan mountains experienced similar phenomena, visible consequences of global warming. In hindsight, 2019 was considered the "year of climate awareness." So it was, for me as well.

We could no longer continue as before.

At that time, I was caught up in a storm of inner tsunami, one of those moments where everything you've experienced gradually falls into place after simmering for a long time. Alongside Emmanuel Faber at Danone, I was witnessing the impact that a massive company can have when it decides to change its ways of thinking and operating. Now I know that we were laying the groundwork for a new model that would seek to move beyond profit-focus and find a new balance. Back then, I was also working with the Consumer Goods Forum (CGF), co-chairing the Collaboration for Healthier Lives initiative. The CGF is an organization which gathers the leaders of 400 industrial groups to drive discussions about how they can collectively make their models more sustainable. It was during a CGF board meeting in November 2019 that I had an awakening. Previously, committed leaders pushing for change were a minority. But that day, I witnessed a shift—those once isolated leaders were becoming the majority. It was a tipping point. Our planet was burning, there was no plan B. The majority of the 58 CEOs present understood that sustainability had to take a central place in their business model and that they no longer had a choice: it was time to roll up their sleeves. The CGF was transforming from a think-tank into a true *act-tank*.

That same year, the climate crisis claimed its first victim in the stock market. The American electricity giant Pacific Gas & Electric Company went bankrupt following deadly fires caused by its high-voltage lines in California. Within weeks, a report from the IPCC (Intergovernmental Panel on Climate Change) prompted 300 companies to reduce their greenhouse gas emissions to keep global warming below 2°C, based on the definition of "reduction targets" by the Science Based Targets initiative. In France, the PACTE law passed. It acted as a formal acknowledgment of the societal role played by companies by creating the *mission-driven company** label which included major criteria as social impact and *purpose**. Every company was being invited to officially contribute to change.

However, at the same time, another pressing, unsettling question was emerging for me: could the two models, the one we had inherited and the one we envisioned, coexist? Could we use both shareholder and stakeholder logic, hierarchical management in some cases, and collaborative management in others? And if not, how could we transition from one model to the other? How could each company, especially the larger ones, become full-fledged change agents without facing any significant consequence?

I believe we are entering a new era: conscious leaders are becoming a movement, not a niche. They are eager to fulfil a role that goes beyond creating financial and economic wealth and to contribute tangibly and visibly to improving people's lives in all aspects.

From the emergence of *Environmental, Social and Governance** (ESG)

The best way to predict the future is to **CREATE IT**.

PETER DRUCKER

norms for analyzing companies' non-financial data to the creation of a legal framework for *purpose-led companies**, there is now a shared belief that a company can serve the common good. What was once a faint hope has now become progressively accepted because it is rooted in economic, managerial, and societal realities. Nowadays, all companies are striving to demonstrate their contribution to the common good, regardless of their size, core business, or areas of activity.

It's no longer just about mitigating the negative consequences of our traditional economic system. Although CSR policies advocate on behalf of this crucial mission to do better business, they fall short. For instance, consider Globescan's recent ranking of the most sustainable companies. Philip Morris is a top performer. However, these ratings lose their meaning and value when we dig deeper to inquire about the company's positive impact. Philip Morris may have sustainable sourcing and likely has strong diverse and inclusive people practices, but it is only natural to wonder what a cigarette manufacturer's actual contribution to society is.

A whole new system needs to be invented, new practices established, to create an inherently virtuous consumption chain. This is the core challenge of using business as a force for good. I am committed to this cause and to helping all those looking for solutions. We are experiencing the beginnings of a revolution driven by conscious consumers who endorse initiatives such as Yuka or Too Good To Go and participate in global marches for the planet.

Compelled by engaged citizens, companies no longer have a choice. The time for action has come. What remains is for these vast machine-like organizations to make the same journey from the head to the heart as the conscious activists who have understood its urgency. Many leaders of the economic and political sectors, from civil society and academia alike, agree that a system on the brink of collapse, damaging the planet and endangering communities, needs reform. But the current challenge is to make this new model operational. Ultimately, the question is no longer "why change?" but rather "how to change?"

EMBRACE YOUR AUTHENTIC SELF

Antoine de Saint-Exupéry, a prominent figure in my upbringing and the brilliant author of *The Little Prince*, once confessed: "I once had little esteem for grown-ups. I was wrong. One never grows up." I find resonance in his words, reflecting on how my own journey has been shaped by such insights. Encountering visionary leaders has indeed broadened my perspective, reinforcing the idea that growth and learning continue throughout life. The values instilled in me since childhood never melt away, helping me navigate this ongoing journey with clarity and purpose. In my family, I learned from an early age to always strive for improvement, to go the extra mile, whether it meant learning new languages, engaging in sports, or excelling at school. I learned to turn challenges into opportunities, to remain resilient, and to make a realistic assessment of my environment. It was during these formative years that I began to grasp what a leader should be: someone who understands their ecosystem, sets a course and a strategy, and empowers others to join them in their progression for growth. A leader needs no courtiers: they need committed individuals who challenge them. This is how pioneers advance, how visionaries spread their wings. I'm more convinced that we're driven from a very young age to shuffle the hands we're dealt, to create new models, to find new methods and processes. My great-grandfather: Edmond Locard, was the father of the modern police system, having founded in 1910 the first forensic science department in the world. I have inherited from him and others a certain appetite for learning directly from experts and a particular admiration for pioneers, entrepreneurs, and front runners who dare to shift paradigms and lead others — often against the current. Always in the name of a higher cause, a mission greater than oneself. For my ancestor, it was about making France safer. For me, it's about turning companies into an engine of paradigm shifts.

However, I can also trace this back to another pivotal episode in my life. Fueled by a thirst for adventure into vast landscapes, I asked my parents to let me travel alone to the United States at the age of 14 and attend high school there. I didn't know the family I was going to live with for a year. Of course, I had imagined landing in California or Florida, living the life of a Hollywood star. Instead, I ended up in Michigan. Looking back, I know it was the best thing that could have happened to me because I experienced something fundamental: a sense of community. We all have certain iconic images in mind of the quintessential American way of life one may be tempted to smile condescendingly at the frequent barbecues, the solemn rendition of the national anthem at every opportunity, the flags fluttering in the yards of posh suburbs and picturesque ranches. Yet, there is a spirit of community to be found there; and it is put in the service of a greater good which transcends our individual existences and compels us towards unity. I wanted to bring certain aspects of this American life back to France — such as taking care of one's community, loving one's country, and embracing shared moments.

Lastly, who I am today has also been shaped by the open-mindedness and kindness of heart which I have been taught — essential qualities for engaging with individuals outside of one's usual circles. When I was sent to England at a young age to learn English, I discovered not only a new language but also families that were quite different from mine, who had struck a different balance through other ways of thinking and living. The same happened when, during my studies, I spent time in Germany.

This openness is also vital for me when it comes to taking risks and venturing forth. "What's holding you back?" a strong and compassionate woman once asked me. Reflecting on it now, I realize I was still bound by old patterns. Or perhaps it was the fear that one experiences while descending a seemingly endless mountain trail on a mountain bike? Regardless, every day, I strive to cultivate openness to the vast world and a taste for adventure because these are essential attitudes for those who want to change the world — no pressure!

MY PERSONAL UNIVERSE

I have five children at home. I want to be able to look them in the eyes and tell them that I have done everything I can to leave them a sustainable world which allows them to believe in their dreams. I keep telling them that everything is possible — or rather, that nothing is impossible. I show them that they don't have to choose between a fulfilling family life and an exciting career; on the contrary, one nourishes the other. And to recharge, nourish my aspirations, and validate my convictions, I often retreat to an alpine chalet in the Beaufortain valley with my husband, a contagiously optimistic entrepreneur who supports me in everything I do.

In my personal galaxy, there are also those guiding stars that led me in my early career steps. The first one would be Jacky Abecassis, who I met when I joined Boiron at the age of 23. One summer, we had to react quickly as an aggressive competitor was aiming to seize the market. I volunteered and, together with him, set up an innovative approach to democratize homeopathy. As a result, in just a few months, we doubled our growth. I was later entrusted with the American market, a massive challenge. We needed to find a way for Boiron, a family-owned company, to establish a presence in a vast market and to make homeopathy acceptable in a country that sold painkillers alongside salads! By fostering partnerships with major distributors and even plastic surgeons, our efforts paid off.

Thierry Boiron was another figure who left a lasting impact on my life. He would often say, "Aim for the moon, because even if you miss, you'll land among the stars" — a quote attributed to Oscar Wilde. I always took this injunction seriously: aim far, aim high, fall, get hurt, rise again, and gradually create your own galaxy of inspiring people.

And so, year after year, I keep discovering precious initiatives that shine like stars. At APRIL, working alongside Bruno Rousset, I learned what it means to be a courageous entrepreneur and visionary. I understood what it means to take risks as well as the power of collaboration. My mission

"

BE THE
CHANGE
YOU WANT
TO SEE
IN THE WORLD

MAHATMA GHANDI

was to set up the company's international division; I did so by establishing a new model taking our growth from 3% to 20% by developing a network of entrepreneurs in 36 countries. Instead of losing ourselves in various projects, we decided to focus on the health of mobile individuals. To do so, we created seven startups and acquired twelve other companies to tackle the issue head-on. Through this process, I discovered the strength of a network of leaders who strive to go further together.

Similarly, there's much to say about the great adventure I experienced at Danone alongside Emmanuel Faber. Large companies have the potential to change the lives of millions, or even billions, of people. They are essential levers, prominent players. They are the drivers and measurers of change. They set the pace and, most importantly, have the necessary scale to change the rules of the game, albeit on one condition: being team-players.

This is my Milky Way, the inner sanctum I come back to before setting out to explore new universes. A path paved with adventures, sewn with hopes, and strewn with obstacles. I have stumbled — often. But at every crossroads, I encountered solid and generous men and women who helped me get back up.

LEARNING THE HARD WAY (SOMETIMES)

Being aware of the imperative to change does not mean no challenges will arise. Progress is often found in the right balance of old ways and new models. Like a cyclist standing up on the pedals to ascend a steep pass, to elevate the whole structure and carry all employees, a leader must contend with gravity, resistance, and the proximity of the summit. Or like a sailor setting out on the water in a dinghy, one must maintain one's course while dealing with the power of the wind, the swell, the lean, the weight of the boat, and the force of their fellow sailor leaning out on the trapeze.

Throughout my professional experiences, I've learned what remains to be done and what is no longer viable. In my view, a company can no longer avoid addressing social and environmental issues or maintain a narrow hiring perspective. Moreover, these two imperatives seem interconnected, as most young graduates express a desire to work a meaningful job and evolve within a company that aims to improve the lives of the people it serves. Among characteristics unique to old corporate cultures, we must also address the women's roles within companies, pay gaps, and the pressure on mothers who, like me, refuse to choose between a fulfilling family life and an exciting professional one.

You can choose courage, or you can choose comfort, but you cannot choose both.

BRENÉ BROWN

Of course, there's the issue of harassment, which many women, including myself, have experienced. This is the first time I'm talking about it publicly. Long before joining men like Bruno Rousset and Emmanuel Faber, I was the target of a man's continuous sexual harassment. I stood up for myself; but when he realized he would not get what he wanted, he pivoted to psychological harassment, repeated humiliations, insults. I couldn't speak about it. I was young and stunned. I kept telling myself, "Your career will be ruined if you confront him." I felt powerless because I was raised to respect authority, admire leaders, and trust those in positions of power. In recent years, voices have started to be heard. I now regret not filing a complaint. But at the time, I feared the potential consequences a report would have on my life, my family, my career.

DON'T SETTLE, SHOOT FOR THE MOON

When I was 20 years old, a young cousin of mine had been battling for years a disease that would ultimately claim his life. Even today, I can't help but shed tears when recalling the question, he asked us (those who knew it might be the last time we would ever see him), a question I will never forget: "What would you like people to say about you at your funeral?" A challenging question, especially for a twenty-year-old. One responded, "that I was a super nice person." Another said, "that I was a good, loving mother to my family and those around me." But when it was my turn to answer, I said: "like you, I would like them to mention that I was a kind and loving person. But I would also like them to say that I made a difference, that I helped move the boundaries for a better world on my own scale." It wasn't just an intuitive answer, it was a genuine one.

So, ever since then, I have wanted to embrace the world in its entirety and contribute to improving the lives of as many people as possible. That is the North star on my personal as well as professional compass, at *Goodness** & Co. Because today, to be chosen, companies must demonstrate their contribution and positive impact on the world. By "being chosen", I do not merely refer to consumer endorsement. It also means convincing investors and attracting talented people by demonstrating that your model contributes to social, environmental, and technological progress in the broadest and deepest sense of human advancement.

More specifically, at the heart of impact-driven companies, there are always men and women of action who are aware of the new demands brought by a new era. People who have chosen to lead whichever transitions are necessary. With these words, I also aim to bear witness to them, to acknowledge and publicize their long-term work — which is like that of a sculptor revealing the new face of 21st-century companies from the clay of everyday life.

I think of all the activists, committed leaders, stakeholders, and colleagues

I work with and who help me grow. I think of all those who want to change the world, regardless of their position, who want to fight for a fairer, more sustainable world. A more human world. These new leaders aren't always in the executive rooms but stand at the doorstep of economic power. This activism isn't ideological; it's primarily economic, managerial, and societal. It isn't rooted in opposition but in the defense of a single cause: progress. Without these leaders, without these people, these catalysts of change, the world would continue to tumble down a slippery slope.

If you're wondering how to make a concrete, daily contribution to this new era of change through actionable pathways within a company, you're in the right place. I certainly don't have a magical wand to offer, because precisely there's no single way to address significant societal challenges. However, I'll strive to present some key principles and experiences that have already proven themselves.

Enjoy!

Within these pages, you will find the keys to transforming your business into a force for good. This framework, the *Goodness Compass*, is a tool for courageous leaders eager to make the shift happen at the core of businesses. It will guide you on the essential steps needed to set your vision and commitments, who to engage in your journey, and how to turn words into actions.

At the heart of the *Goodness Compass* lies the three pillars of building business as a force for good:

IMAGINE: Craft a vision that's more than just a dream — make it a mission with purpose and commitment. This is where you define what you stand for.

ENGAGE: Rally your people! Whether it's your team, customers, or partners, everyone plays a role in turning your vision into reality. No vision takes flight without the right crew to help you carry the torch.

ACT: Time to walk the talk! Take meaningful steps toward change through innovation, inclusivity, and aligning your operating model with your mission. The real magic happens here — where big ideas meet bold action, where businesses put their values into practice and make change happen.

SEE THE GOOD, Some days you just have to **CREATE YOUR OWN SUNSHINE**.

Your thoughts and internal world is what's creating your external world. The happiness of your life depends on the quality of your thoughts. **Whatever you put focus on expands**. So train your mind to see the good in everything.

POSITIVITY IS A CHOICE.

1.
IMAGINE

Imagine being a force for good

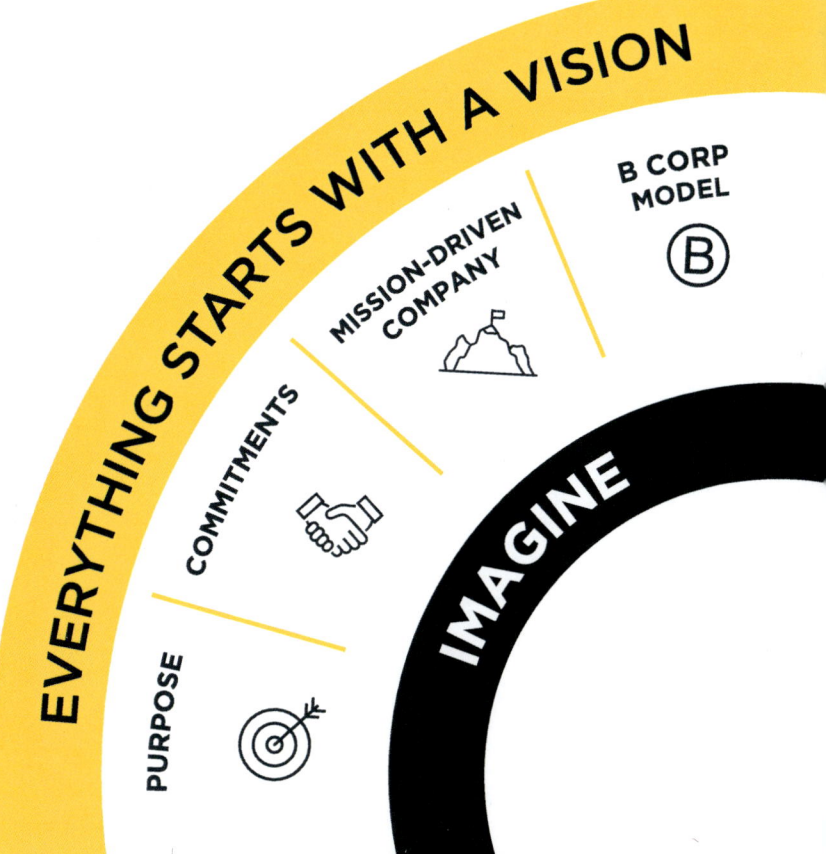

EVERYTHING STARTS WITH A VISION

PURPOSE

COMMITMENTS

MISSION-DRIVEN COMPANY

B CORP MODEL

B

IMAGINE

Just as a sailor plans their journey and carefully studies navigation charts, every business envisions a long-term trajectory and considers the consequences of its path. While it's common to establish financial projections, what about social and environmental projections? In this first part, I want to discuss the changes I have witnessed within certain companies and society. While such alarm bells as the IPCC's latest report (which stresses the need for an ecological awakening within the next three years) are being rung, it seems that our collective awareness is growing at an accelerating rate; meanwhile, companies can and must lead changes within our production, consumption, and action model.

It would be incorrect to assume that 20th-century companies were oblivious to their ecosystem. On the contrary, many of them committed to causes through their foundations or philanthropic endeavors — which in France has been greatly encouraged since the 2003 Aillagon law has made it possible for it to be rewarded with a 60% deduction on Corporate Income Tax.[2] This model was then followed up by the CSR generation, whose primary aim is to limit companies' negative environmental and social output. As we were growing aware of the limits it behooves us to put on resource exploitation, we also witnessed the emergence of new ways of assessing the tangible consequences of our activities on the planet and human communities. To go even further, it's time to transition towards an impact-driven business model which would make its contribution to progress an integral part of its DNA. This is the 21st-century model I will discuss in this first chapter.

PURPOSE-LED
COMPANY

The wealth of the 5 richest men has doubled since 2020, while 5 billion people have become poorer[3], where between 4.8 and 12.7 million tons of plastic pieces are dumped into the ocean each year[4], and where the global population of wild animals has dropped by 69% on average since 1970[5], it's undeniable that it is no longer viable or even desirable to keep defining growth purely from a financial standpoint. 73% of leaders acknowledge this fact, according to the KPMG's 2023 CEO Outlook, yet most of them struggle to envision an alternative growth strategy.[6]

Furthermore, given that companies have the means to act, it's natural for citizens to expect them to be at the forefront of change – not merely waiting for regulations to be imposed (which also vary significantly from one country to another) but actively driving progress. The Edelman Trust Barometer reflects this trend: eight out of ten people seem to consider that companies, especially their leaders, should be proactive in suggesting solutions and taking responsibilities — as well as being held accountable when they fail in their mission.[7] This sentiment is reflected in France's PACTE Law, which modified Article 1835 of the Civil Code to state that "companies should go beyond pursuing profit. A company must be a place for creating shared value."

WALK THE WALK

Moreover, it seems that young graduates no longer wish to work for companies that don't demonstrate a true commitment to society and environmental preservation through an ambitious sustainability strategy. According to the same survey, around 62% of them would decline a job offer from a company not adequately engaged in these matters.[8] Conversely, companies with significant sustainability programs are said to experience up to 13% more profits annually than their counterparts.[9]

This growing expectation from the workforce reflects a broader trend: although the role of private actors in society is now recognized by most leaders worldwide, there's still much to be invented and implemented in practice. A significant gap persists between rhetoric and action. My intention is not to indulge in mere wishful thinking but, on the contrary, to contemplate how to measure the positive impact of companies on the society they operate in, utilizing Key Performance Indicators (KPIs) and always following a collectively developed roadmap. In other words, among the crucial principles for instigating and supporting this model change, it's imperative to keep in mind how impact-focused companies can generate not only wealth but also economic, social, and environmental value.

ACTIVISM IN BUSINESS

As companies are now expected to demonstrate their contribution to societal well-being, the decision to embrace this paradigmatic shift often falls on the CEOs' shoulders, although they're not the sole players in this decision — which I will discuss further later. It's vital that all individuals in positions of power internalize this truth: impact doesn't come at the expense of profit. In fact, its proven than that the cost of inaction is higher than the cost of action. Numerous concrete examples have proven it.

For instance, since 1973, Patagonia has proudly declared that "[they are] in business to save our home planet." Its founders, passionate athletes

and nature lovers, have put environmental activism at the core of their company's DNA. Since its inception, this brand – whose garments are made from 87% recycled materials – has continually redefined its business model to minimize its production's environmental impact. Founder Yvon Chouinard emphasized in his 2005 bestseller *Let My People Go Surfing: The Education of a Reluctant Businessman* that "you can't wait for all the answers before taking action." It's a mindset that I also aim to cultivate – this willingness they displayed, well ahead of anyone else, to transcend the competitive mindset and to recognize that global challenges are shared by all. Instead, Patagonia shared its innovations and created a platform that somewhat resembles an associative Tinder, connecting NGOs with environmental volunteers. The world also remembers their 2011 campaign "Don't Buy This Jacket", which was a protest the consumerism associated with Black Friday and its disastrous environmental impact. Ultimately, in the founders' view, a purchase is equivalent to a vote, and environmental activism is the essence of the company's culture.

In the guidance I provide to companies undergoing transformation, I often advise them to begin by clearly defining their vision for the future. Three questions can help in defining this mindset and the subsequent guiding actions. First, I ask them to identify the major social issues that hold particular significance to employees, clients, partners, and the ecosystem in which the company operates. The second question concerns current business opportunities, markets, trends, as well as consumer habits; how can these be seen through the lens of *early makers*, i.e. the pioneers who can anticipate shifts and disruptions in collective habits? Thirdly, I push them to reflect on the company's specific attributes. In what area could we have the most impact? What strengths do we possess? What expertise have we gained? By answering these questions, leaders can identify a playing field in which they hold unique legitimacy.

I call this the company's IKIGAÏ. This Japanese concept, which helps individuals identify their needs, strengths, and available opportunities, also reveals something about a company's DNA and, more importantly, provides insight into the best way to initiate the transition from a traditional model to that of an impact-driven enterprise, explicitly defining its purpose.

PURPOSE AS A NORTH STAR

Purpose has become the word on everyone's lips, and that's a wonderful thing. However, it's crucial to understand how to define it and, most importantly, what to do once that conceptual work is completed. On this topic, Jean-Dominique Senard explains that the concept of purpose "captures in a single phrase what gives meaning to the collective goal of the company." He adds that "purpose consists in bringing ourselves back to the social object in the original sense of the term, as in the early days of the Limited Company, when its goal was focused on public interest." This notion of public interest or common good, is seemingly outdated in our contemporary context. However, it perfectly encapsulates how every company should care for the world it's part of – not as a spectator or, worse, a profiteer, but as an actor bearing the same responsibilities as any inhabitant of the world. The idea that businesses can integrate the common good in aiming for higher performance is no longer a dream.

What's true for small businesses might even be more so for larger ones. Let me explain. It was in 2012, during a discussion in a Lyon café with serial entrepreneur Bruno Bonnel (who is now leading the investment fund Plan France 2030), that I fully grasped the overwhelming impact of multinational corporation on society. I particularly understood how much they can influence the planet's and its inhabitants' well-being. Until then, I had been more drawn to small-scale businesses, thinking that they were the place where I could exert the most immediate personal influence. And yet, Bruno (who has significantly guided me throughout my career) pointed out that, within a group, I could impact billions of people.

So, I decided to take the plunge. I aimed for the moon, striving to steer

PURPOSE is a powerful motivator. The companies that will thrive will be those that will **STEP UP** to address the big challenges facing society.

INDRA NOOYI

the world in the right direction. That's why I chose to join Danone. I often say that I was "thirsty for impact." Given the unprecedented challenges of our times, I wanted to be part of a multinational corporation with the capacity to act on a large scale – especially since, under the leadership of Antoine Riboud and his son Franck, Danone had already decided that there could be no trade-off between economic and social progress. It had to be all or nothing, through the choice of good products that "bring health through nutrition to as many people as possible" (Charter on Food, Nutrition, and Health).

DANONE: A CASE STUDY

At Danone, I immediately encountered individuals driven by an intra-preneurial logic, people who were committed to building a future model on solid foundations. This approach empowers employees and colleagues to be change makers, whatever their role or level in the organization, with their unique talents and creativity. While reading Emmanuel Faber's *Paths to Change*, I found a clear verbalization of intuitions that had been swirling around my mind for a long time. For instance, the idea that "an economic decision that doesn't consider its social dimension would be barbaric, and a social action that doesn't consider its economic dimension would be utopian. Social and economic aspects have been pitted against each other, but they are facets of a single reality. The boundary between the two passes through our consciousness." This, succinctly expressed, is the posture we need to adopt to implement positive change through conscious activism.

Therefore, I wanted to join Danone because I believed in the tremendous positive impact that the company (and hence its members) could make on the world. Alongside Emmanuel Faber, the company developed its commitment based on the participation of its entire team. Together, we launched the 2030 "One Planet One Health" strategy, built around nine objectives. Those were split into three leading principles. The first one concerns "the business model"; based on the *B Corp*™* certification, it aims to continuously innovate and generate superior, sustainable, and profitable growth. The second dimension of the 2030 strategy concerns "the brand model". The brand-related objectives involve brands promoting good health everywhere, every day and engaging them to preserve the planet and renew its resources. The third dimension is named "the trust model". It involves entrusting the future to the teams, promoting inclusive growth, and rallying around the food revolution. The nine objectives within Danone's core guiding principles are aligned with the United Nations' Sustainable Development Goals.

Since 2018, each of Danone's 100,000 employees has been invited to contribute to shaping this roadmap and evaluating its efficiency within their specific roles, departments, and divisions. This takes concrete shape through the "One Person, One Voice, One Action" program, which relies on a digital platform offering in-depth training modules related to the company's vision and objectives as well as on a commitment to co-constructing the company's strategy over time.

To have
DETERMINATION,
DRIVE and
COURAGE to
push through
any challenge
or obstacle
thrown your way
until you
succeed.

NELSON MANDELA

Emmanuel FABER, Chair, The ISSB Board and Former CEO & Chair, Danone

Before I decided to join Danone, in 2012, I read the book of Emmanuel "Chemins de traverse". At that moment, I knew right away that Emmanuel was going to be the courageous leader that the world needed. I'm so grateful for our journey together at Danone.

"We need leaders who want to change the game. The world can only change if companies become activists. In this increasingly complex world, companies are being fundamentally challenged to determine whom they truly serve. It is important for companies to answer this question of intent and purpose in clear, simple terms. It's the best way to restore trust from employees, consumers, partners, civil society, and governments. Change takes time, of course. Large companies operate under financial constraints. And, most importantly, for change to happen there needs to be individual awareness. Organizations don't convert to new realities; individuals do. We need leaders who, at some point, want to make a difference. It's also time for us to work on developing standards that enable all economic actors to reconcile economic performance and impact."

PURPOSE IN ACTION
WHAT IF?

What is your company's purpose beyond profit? To address this question, you can think about your company's IKIGAÏ, its reason to be.

- What are the main challenges our society is facing that your company can address?

- What are your growth perspectives when it comes to sustainable business?

- What resonates with your stakeholders' expectations where you are legitimate to act?

If your dreams
don't scare you,
they're not
big enough.

RICHARD BRANSON

VISION, AMBITION, **AND COMMITMENTS**

When it comes to change, it's all about leadership. All it takes is for the right person with great force of conviction for an economic model to become socially and financially virtuous.

THE POSITIVE IMPACT REVOLUTION

In recent decades, we've become aware of the necessity to protect our planet and the role that business can play in this mission. ESG matters have become more central, aiming to reduce companies' negative footprint and limit risks. Companies have already made enormous efforts in this area. But we're now at a tipping point, where they must reinvent their model to prove the positive contribution they can make to society. This is what I call the positive impact revolution. Today, companies must not only limit their negative output but also prove their net positive contribution. They need to rethink their model, assuming they can choose to promote or discontinue certain activities based on their impact on the world.

After trying to "do more by doing less", our current challenge is to build a regenerative economy*, i.e. an economic system that operates in service to life, strengthening the vitality of the natural and social systems that the economy is also ultimately dependent on. In a nutshell, the time has come to invent companies which positively contribute to social progress while still creating wealth for shareholders and value for all stakeholders — from suppliers to consumers.

A VISION AT THE CORE

What Paul Polman, former CEO of Unilever (2009-2019), has demonstrated through his strategy – which I encountered at the Consumer Goods Forum and through the IMAGINE project – is that a strong vision gives profound meaning to action. Ahead of his time, Polman believed that any future business growth would have to be rooted in sustainability and responsibility. In 2010, he launched the Unilever Sustainable Living Plan to set a standard for sustainable living by identifying the key issues which a company could address due to their alignment with its DNA. These issues include the state of the planet, the well-being and trust of individuals, as well as social inclusion. His successor Alan Jope, as a pragmatic and determined leader, has reinforced the role of companies in shaping the future and concretized this vision further by aligning transformation in categories, brands, and geographical expansion with major sustainability goals. Alan believes that the trade-off paradigm is a misconception: we should not have to choose between profit and impact. This is only common sense: prosperity entails caring for employees, treating partners with respect, ensuring the well-being of customers and consumers, and positively impacting the communities in which we operate. Profit will follow naturally. To overcome the organizational paralysis caused by this supposed paradox, it is highly useful to connect the business case with tangible signs. Will his successor Hein Schumacher carry the legacy?

Unilever's case illustrates this: the group's activist brands have seen six times greater growth and €1.2 billion savings due to sustainable sourcing and its clear strategy for attracting new talents.[10] Over a decade, Unilever has become the preferred employer in its sector in 52 out of the 54 countries where it operates, compared to 17 countries a decade ago. In the era of the talent war, this is a strong sign of competitiveness. The company's CSO, Rebecca Marmot, has played an important role in this strategy while also bringing her deep insight into the question of women's roles in business. She believes sustainability is at the core of business success:

demonstrating growth, establishing trust, reducing risks, or cutting costs. Adopting sustainable practices amplifies this approach throughout the value chain, within your own organization. It means acting through your brands. It involves pushing for policy change. This is how we demonstrate a direct link with business, with the company's economic performance.

For me, such leaders are the visionaries we need — the ones who are conscious of their responsibilities and their company's impact, who set ambitious goals for the common good. Purpose acts as a compass which everyone can use to measure their decisions against social and environmental commitments. But remember, use actual performance indicators — otherwise, this is just a wish list!

COMMIT! (AND SET QUANTIFIABLE GOALS)

There will be no climate justice without social *justice**. We are all familiar with the major themes which the United Nations have defined through their seventeen Sustainable Development Goals. Depending on your activity, some SDGs may be more familiar to you than others. The SDGs, as far as the planet is concerned, involve nature and *biodiversity** protection, climate-related commitments, and *circular economy** practices to conserve resources are key. As Saint-Exupéry said and I often quote, "we do not inherit the Earth. We borrow it from our children." And we are the generation that knows. We have lost 80% of insects in the last 30 years in Europe.[11] If we add two more degrees to the current global warming, coral reefs will disappear.[12] There is a sense of urgency. When it comes to people, our commitments range from diversity and inclusion policies to workplace well-being. In regard to communities, the most fundamental aspects are those of human rights, working conditions, and fair wages. The challenges are immense and becoming more urgent each year.

The second-hand luxury market has expanded, from €26 billion in 2021 to €35 billion in 2024. It has grown five times faster than new luxury sales over the same period.[13] Kering, under the leadership of Marie-Claire Daveu, is an inspiration which shows that sustainability is a driver of value creation. With its "Crafting Tomorrow's Luxury" strategy, Kering has committed to reducing its greenhouse gas emissions by 40% by 2035.[14] This requires new ways to act and make decisions. To guide their strategic decisions, Kering has been a pioneer with an innovative tool to measure and quantify the environmental impact of its activities: the Environmental Profit & Loss account. To foster breakthrough innovation across the value chain, Kering, in collaboration with Gucci, has launched the first circular hub in Italy.

FROM WORDS TO ACTIONS

Progress is made. Sustainability is now firmly on the corporate agenda. While a handful or organizations had carbon reduction goals a decade ago, today two-thirds of Fortune Global 500 companies have significant ESG commitments today.[15] The shift is happening. Business leaders must be prepared to adapt their business models to the evolving regulatory landscape, particularly in the European Union where the requirements of the Corporate Sustainability Reporting Directive (CSRD) will gradually apply to nearly all companies over time. Its implementation will result in increased transparency, reliability and comparability among company stakeholders. The regulation will not only concern big companies but also medium-sized ones.

Therefore, every company leader should ask themselves: what can I act on? Where can I make a difference based on my company's history, its industry, its closest concerns, and my employees' considerations? Once priorities are established, we make it possible to make commitments that act as navigation guides. Achieving each goal will likely require adjusting the pace depending on circumstances: slow down during storms, accelerate in fair weather. The courage* of leaders also provide the necessary momentum.

No single company is expected to "save the world" alone. Regarding each aspect of the ESG commitments — as defined in the United Nations' Sustainable Development Goals, established in 2015 and consolidated in the 2030 Agenda — it's crucial to find guidance from precise, quantifiable objectives. I maintain that commitment without KPIs, evaluations, and numbers resembles a prayer more than a roadmap. Despite numerous references and standards now available to guide companies in advancing and assessing their progress based on ESG criteria — such as Ecovadis, UN Global Compact, Global Reporting Initiative, CPD, and ISO — navigating these requirements remains challenging. In early 2024, more than 200 companies had their Net-Zero commitments "removed" by the Science Based Targets initiative (SBTi). 80% of these companies had joined the campaign primarily to demonstrate leadership in sustainability and later admitted to having "lost track" of their pledges.[16] Companies must begin with the unique challenges inherent to their specific missions. Clarifying how these objectives can be achieved is the most critical part of the roadmap. Yet, while many companies have adopted carbon neutrality commitments, 55% admit to lacking concrete plans. It's necessary, above all, to understand the playing field and the expectations of one's stakeholders. This is what's known as the materiality matrix, which lists what truly matters to employees, suppliers, investors, etc. Is it world hunger, data protection, business ethics? Ultimately, how well a company engages with all these actors depends on the level of attention it pays to their objectives and how effectively it aligns their efforts.

I deeply appreciate what IKEA has done for instance. The company, for which "sustainability is business", adopted a strategy based on three pillars: sustainable and healthy living spaces, circularity in operations, and planet protection. Workplace equality and fairness also heavily come into play. Each of these broad objectives translates into a variety of specific actions and solutions, following a strict agenda. Consider IKEA's commitment to circular operations through recycled materials and on-site renewable energy, among other efforts. The company also has an ambitious goal: to increase its activity while halving its greenhouse gas emissions. All employees are involved in this major project in various ways.

STAYING THE COURSE

According to the American philosopher Ralph Waldo Emerson "it is not the destination, it's the journey". Establishing the roadmap — without playing on words — is somewhat similar. Regardless, the only way to implement and integrate a company's objectives is to develop them with the right people.

To earnestly guide the company towards its intended course, I recommend putting together a committee composed of stakeholders, sustainability issue experts, company leaders, and heads of cross-functional teams like communication or innovation — in a one-third ratio for each category. This committee, however, doesn't exempt the company from regularly involving external stakeholders and all employees, because understanding viewpoints and potentially adjusting strategies is crucial for accuracy.

Denis MACHUEL, CEO, The Adecco Group

With leadership comes responsibility. This is very true for Denis who leads with head and heart in fast-paced and challenging contexts. A strong advocate of diversity and inclusion, Denis was meant to be a leader of people-focused businesses.

"What incentive do we have to focus on sustainability in the first place? There are probably as many defenders of Milton Friedman as there are advocates of companies playing a societal role out there. And, recently, economic tensions have tended to strengthen the Friedmanians. So, my advice to a business leader who would like to strengthen their commitments is the following: if you are not deeply convinced and ready to fight, don't even try. But if you are, then the only way to make sustainability a part of your business is to embed it deeply in your business practices — in an almost symbiotic way.

Opponents of sustainability or stakeholders who are not convinced will always try to demonstrate that it is a mere gimmick which will weaken the business. I've heard countless comments along those lines: "you're spreading yourself too thin!", "are we sure it's going to have a real impact?", "is it a priority?", "it will threaten financial performance, when the investors want to see a return on their investment!"

The only way forward is to remain anchored in your convictions and to prove your thesis with facts: the effective combination of economic performance and sustainability is at the heart of business. And there is little point in proclaiming it; the best way to demonstrate it is through the tangible efficiency of business, because that is irrefutable proof. Starting by doing it in the shadows avoids the risk of falling into greenwashing and allows you to calibrate your efforts and better target your actions. Once that's done, you can accelerate and scale up.

If it's isolated or disconnected from the core business, sustainability ends up dying, due to a lack of funding or engagement fatigue. If it is anchored at the heart of the company's business, it proves its relevance and engages employees properly."

COMMITMENTS IN ACTION
WHAT IF?

- What are your commitments regarding nature protection and well-being of individuals and communities?

- What criteria, beyond economics, measure and guide your performance?

- How can these ESG commitments be translated into concrete actions?

THE MISSION-DRIVEN
COMPANY

If anyone still had any doubts regarding the extent of the changes we are experiencing, they would need only to open the French Civil Code to Article 1833, as recently modified by the PACTE law. Since 2019, the law recognizes the obligation for companies to take societal and environmental issues into account in their activities.

The PACTE law also allows the most earnest companies to include a purpose statement in their bylaws. This is far from insignificant, as it provides a clear explanation of how a company contributes to and impacts the broader society in which it operates. The concept of purpose is no longer just a vague "inspiring" roadmap, but truly a set of actions outlining a concrete contribution to society. To put it into perspective, it's a bit like a political party having to state in a few sentences the ultimate reason for its existence.

A mission statement acts as a framework, creating expectations from stakeholders, be it consumers or employees. It is also a way to build a competitive edge. During the Covid-19 crisis, Bank of America calculated that the most socially engaged companies had five to ten points higher in the stock market than their counterparts.[17]

A BIG STEP FOR FRANCE (AND THE WORLD)

The PACTE law created the Mission-Driven Company (*Entreprise* à Mission) status (as per the French Commercial Code, Article 210-10). It encompasses companies which amend their bylaws to include a mission with purpose as well as concrete commitments to social and environmental objectives. The company must also agree for its *governance* * to be monitored and guided by a Mission Committee that is regularly evaluated by a third-party auditor.

While 75% of French public companies have a stated purpose, only 20% of them have it written in their bylaws. Nearly 1490 companies have already become *Entreprises à Mission*, and several hundred more are in the process of joining the movement.[18] This also means that over 905,000 employees within organizations like Danone, La Banque Postale, Arverne Group, or La Poste, pioneering companies like Clariane, Enedis, Teract, as well as Small to Medium Enterprises (SMEs) like Vever, or Alenvi, are now actively engaged in transforming traditional business models. The mission-driven company label is a formal acknowledgment of the societal role a company wants to play. As a legal status, it also acts as a badge of trust for consumers and partners, while more effectively attracting new talents.

At Danone, I quickly witnessed the effects of this choice when we gained twenty preference points among students over just a few months. For me, the transition to a mission-driven company is a collective journey, a unique opportunity to guide the organization's strategic and operational choices. In a way, it's like a GPS which doubles as a generator of progress. The Entreprise à Mission not only includes its purpose in its bylaws but also outlines the social and environmental objectives it has chosen. The PACTE law also introduced two governance bodies to oversee the achievement of these objectives, making sure they align with the promises outlined in the company's stated purpose. A dedicated independent mission committee is tasked with exclusively overseeing the mission's progress. Comprising at least one employee of the company, it also includes external stakeholders,

Business can be **A FORCE FOR GOOD**. It's time for **CORPORATE ACTIVISM** to lead the way in **SOLVING SOCIETAL CHALLENGES**.

MARC BENIOFF

enabling leadership teams to benefit from rigorous guidance to make coherent choices and actions in line with the targeted objectives. On the other hand, an independent third-party organization is also responsible for verifying that the objectives outlined in the bylaws are effectively achieved and commitments are upheld through regular audits.

Obviously, the *Entreprise à Mission* being a fairly recent initiative, it is not a one-size-fits-all solution. It should be acknowledged that it's a framework within which companies can operate, and the legal implications of such a choice are not trivial. It has existed in Italy and the United States for some time; other countries are developing similar legal frameworks, such as numerous countries in Latin America or, more recently, Spain. But those examples highlight the need for a European legal framework and an international reference model.

CREATING A BETTER WORLD, INSIDE AND OUT

During a session of the Community of Mission-Driven Companies, I met Emery Jacquillat, a man on a mission. Based on the discussions we had and considering his unique journey, I now consider Emery to be the epitome of an enlightened entrepreneur. He hasn't hesitated to take frequent risks to transform his business and fully commits to promoting an impact-driven entrepreneurial model. He took over the leadership of Camif, a mission-driven company selling sustainable, made-in-France interior design projects in 2008 — at a time when such objectives weren't particularly attractive or mainstream.

Even more radically, since 2017, Emery closes the company down on Black Friday to protest overconsumption, despite many companies making staggering profits on the holiday. This virtuous decision has certainly paid off, as the group saw a yearly growth rate of around 44% compared to previous years.19 Because of his ongoing commitment, Emery was the first Chairman of the Community of Mission-Driven Companies.

This phenomenon is also observable in the textile and fashion sector, encouraged especially by the decreasing popularity of fast fashion among consumers. Aigle (which became a mission-driven company in 2021) is a pioneer in the field. This choice was led by Sandrine Conseiller; considering that the biggest risk would be to not take any risks at all. It translated specific objectives for their new collections, to optimize the impact of their products. Aigle also launched a second-hand platform called Second Souffle, which collects and promotes second-hand pieces in its stores.

Ultimately, it seems that the ambitious choice to transform a company's bylaws in order to become a mission-driven company results in tangible, measurable actions. An encouraging sign of the ongoing revolution.

This is why I am so happy to see companies in the health industry also moving forward. Most notably, Doctolib (the biggest French platform dedicated to booking medical appointments online) became an *Entreprise à Mission* in 2023. Doctolib has drastically reduced the delays in access to medical care for patients and improved conditions for health workers. 86% of users live outside of the five biggest cities in France; moreover, these are users of all ages, with more than seven million users over the age of 65. The platform is used by over 340,000 healthcare professionals, across all medical fields and all over the territory.[20] Co-founder and CEO Stanislas Niox-Chateau has also announced that he would be investing almost one hundred million euros into the development of innovative solutions for patients and healthcare professionals.[21]

In 2023, listed mission-driven companies are thriving, with numerous new listings on Euronext Paris. OBIZ is one of our favorites, being the first GoodTech company on the stock exchange market. It's a company we admire, led by Brice Chambard, a dedicated leader committed to making business a force for good. OBIZ exemplifies a case for change, demonstrating how economic performance and positive impact can be harmoniously integrated. As a Board member, I've seen the company's efforts firsthand.

Last year, seven subsidiaries of major corporations became mission-driven companies. For instance, Nestlé Health Science France embraced this transformation with its purpose of "empowering healthier lives, today and tomorrow through nutrition." The company set three clear objectives to support this mission. Their efforts to promote prevention and healthier habits are crucial, with their employees actively participating as both beneficiaries and ambassadors.

Emery JACQUILLAT, CEO of Camif and Cofounder, the Community of Mission-Driven Companies

A man on a mission, Emery not only is a very good storyteller, but he is an intuitive, committed and engaged entrepreneur. His boldness and entrepreneurial spirit remind us that it is everyone's duty to become a change maker.

"A good, unique, ambitious mission that is rooted in the company's economic model is a force for transformation for both the company and society. The mission resonates in the hearts of employees, attracting talent and serving as a lever for engagement, innovation, and performance for the company that seizes it. Mission-driven companies decide to bet on love: if we love our planet and our children, we love the company that mobilizes its stakeholders and demonstrates this love by placing positive impact at the core of its economic model to address the challenges of the 21st century."

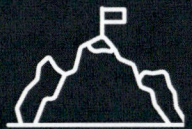

MISSION-DRIVEN COMPANY IN ACTION
WHAT IF?

- Is your company ready to integrate its purpose into its bylaws?

- What would the social and environmental objectives related to your purpose be?

- What about a shift in governance with a mission committee?

- Are you ready for your company's progress to be regularly and thoroughly assessed by a third party?

A movement that changes both **hearts** and **minds** is the greatest kind of **leadership**.

MICHELLE OBAMA

THE B CORP MOVEMENT
AND BEYOND

The B Corp movement is an international movement which unites over 9000 companies of all sizes and from diverse sectors across 102 countries.[22] B Corp companies aim not to be the best in the world, but the best *for* the world. They work towards a shift from a shareholder-based economy to a partnership-based economy which would create value for their ecosystem.

Once upon a time, there was Chloé, the world's first luxury brand to achieve B Corp certification in late 2021. Such a decision demands the bold vision of a leader like Riccardo Bellini, a forward-thinking individual who aims to redefine the rules of his industry. Making the brand grow? Of course. But his ambition was for growth based on a regenerative, impactful model. There is something to be said about the challenge of being the first in your sector to undertake something big. For me, Chloé's commitment to B Corp is a testament to the legacy of a culture established by Gaby Aghion, its founder. A pioneering stylist, she was dedicated to female empowerment from the 1950s onwards. This commitment also reflects the energy of a dedicated collective determined to align the brand with the common good. Under the leadership of Aude Vergne, the Chief Sustainability Officer of the brand, choosing B Corp was a way for the company to engage in a highly demanding journey of progress.

Therefore, the brand now places its contribution to societal challenges at the core of its actions by, for instance, supporting young girls worldwide through the UNICEF Girls Forward program. Beyond being a mere certification to display, the B Corp label commits Chloé to the sustainability of its activities and its impact on society, especially on women.

MEASURING IMPACT

If the purpose-driven company is truly the model for the 21st century, the B Corp movement is one of its standard-bearers, as a community of influential, ambitious peers dedicated to the world and its future. Indeed, the 20th-century economy was shareholder-driven, primarily focused on short-term returns, value extraction, and competition. Contrary to this logic, the B Corp movement demonstrates that the economy of tomorrow will be partnership driven. This means it will be guided by the effects of activities over the long term, the regeneration of exploited resources, and the inclusion of partners from all walks of life. This model is more equitable because shareholders are no longer the sole recipients of value, which now holds various meanings. This is what the B Corp movement and its community of committed leaders advocate for: redefining the rules of the game.

While purpose provides a compass for each company, I see B Corp as a tool that will help keep a focus on environmental and societal objectives. These particularly demanding objectives apply not only to the company's operations but also to how it interacts with all its stakeholders. Unlike the *Entreprise à Mission* — which is tied to a unique and unprecedented legal framework in France and other countries with similar but not identical legislation –, the B Corp movement offers an internationally applicable tool for measuring and managing impact to encourage all companies to do better. Its reference framework, the Business Impact Assessment (BIA), developed by B Lab, precisely and methodically tracks a company's progress in key environmental and social areas, observing the practical implementation of its efforts and their translation among employees, clients, suppliers, and partners. In addition to B Corp-certified companies worldwide, more than 280,000 companies use the BIA as a reference framework to assess their impact and embark on a journey of progress.[23]

As the B Corp label has gained recognition worldwide, becoming a B Corp company indicates the recognition of a company's performance in terms of its impact on the world, its commitment to the common good within its bylaws, and the transparency of its operations. And most importantly, at the heart of this movement and the certification process is what's called the Declaration of Interdependence.

RADICAL INTERDEPENDENCE

The Declaration of Interdependence primarily consists of compelling figures. Nearly one in two B Corp companies acknowledges having established new partnerships with other B Corp companies after joining the movement. What better proof of the interdependence of companies?

More concretely, this declaration encompasses five dimensions integral to any company: governance, employees, community, environment, and clients. The company's evaluation is based on these parameters through the BIA questionnaire, with the score then verified during an audit and eventually formalized for the company to join the community and, ultimately, modify its purpose. Another guarantee is that the label is only valid for three years and must be reappraised by a new audit afterwards. Moreover, it is as of now the world's most demanding label, as the questionnaire's level of detail is incredibly precise. Those who participate in this endeavor must answer over 200 questions ranging from the company's environmental impact to the practical conditions for changing paradigms and opting for a stakeholder-based economy. In a way, the company's maturity is evaluated, along with its ability to concretely address the major challenges of the century.

Among the most well-known B Corp companies, I naturally think of Natura & Co, the largest company to be B Corp certified. The efforts required to attain this label are truly impressive. Today, the three B Corp certified brands under the group — Aésop, Natura, and The Body Shop — have each integrated a primary goal related to their products. Through their 2030 Commitments to Life program, each brand adheres to a very specific set of pledges. One brand focuses on environmental protection, another on human rights, and the last on the circular economy. For Natura & Co, its brands are tools for action, especially towards the empowerment of all women.

WHAT'S NEXT?

Currently somewhat unknown, the B Corp label is, nevertheless, highly valued by both the younger generations and those with strong knowledge of ESG matters. However, while the framework is particularly suited for small companies that can easily aggregate very specific information about their operations and activities, certification remains less straightforward for larger companies. Still, the movement is growing, and bigger companies have been showing interest — which gives me many reasons to hope for a better world.

L'Occitane, a true inspiration when it comes to sustainability at the core of business, recently became a B Corporation. The leadership team embodied by André Hoffmann along with the Geiger father and son duo demonstrated true leadership when it comes to positive change, especially regarding biodiversity. They enthusiastically joined a community of 9000 small, medium and large companies eager to balance profit with purpose.

Sanofi Consumer Healthcare embraced its B Corp journey with the ambition to demonstrate its brand's commitment to better health and certify entities globally. Julie Van Ongevalle envisioned the B Corp model as an integral part of the business roadmap. She believes that everyone has a role to play in contributing to a healthier planet and society.

Rituals is another trailblazer. In an era where businesses are redefining their role in society, Rituals' 25 years' commitment to lead the change is a beacon of hope. Under the leadership of Raymond Cloosterman, the Rituals Profit Pledge was created to restore balance by funding projects that improve the wellbeing of people and planet. The Pledge is a bold initiative, committing to donate 10% of their annual profit to these initiatives that align with their core values of sustainability, well-being, and community support. True success extends beyond the bottom line to include positive societal impact.

B Corp is a movement of leaders for good. We are not alone. Such collective movements are precious. When I recall the formative moments of my life, those moments when suddenly everything becomes clear, one such moment I experienced was in October 2020 in New York. I had been selected along with eleven other women to be part of the inaugural Future Women community organized by B Corp. Whether an entrepreneur or working with an organization, we all came together to share how we envisioned the future of business and, most importantly, the actions required to concretely bring about this new model. At the time, I feared not being up to the task. However, in discussing with these women of conviction and action, I was immediately reassured by the energy, strength, and motivation of such exceptional individuals as Lorna Davis, Rosie Warin, and Victoria Foster.

Marcello PALAZZI, entrepreneur for human progress

Entrepreneur, Marcello Palazzi is the essence of a catalyst, the driving force behind numerous leadership movements. Some people nourish your soul and help you grow. Marcello is this type of leader. Alongside Leen Zevenbergen, he co-founded Good Leaders, a collective aiming to bring together over 30,000 leaders for a regenerative economy, an economy where people and planet thrive.

"As the world finally realizes that the economy and companies

must change to respect both humanity and the planet, regenerating a world that is overheating and overconsuming in its wealthiest regions, a new movement of thousands of B Corp-certified companies, impact-driven companies, Benefit Corporations, impact investment funds, and B leaders is paving the way. Adhering to the highest standards in governance, social, environmental, and human development, the various B Corp tools are used by over 280,000 companies to measure 'performance for the common good' or a positive impact on people and the planet. The movement's goal is not to make every company a B Corp, but to inspire and show that it is entirely possible to succeed financially while respecting people and the planet. These impact-driven companies are often more successful and will become even more so given regulatory requirements, new accounting standards, investor pressure, and societal expectations."

THE B CORP MODEL IN ACTION
WHAT IF?

- Are you willing to rethink the way you lead your business, shifting from a shareholder-oriented logic to a partnership-oriented logic?

- What about analyzing your business model using the Business Impact Assessment (BIA) questionnaire?

- To what extent are you ready to make your governance more transparent?

It's hard to keep an **OPEN MIND** if you don't have an open heart.

ADAM GRANT

2.
ENGAGE WITH HEAD AND HEART

Rallying allies through more inclusive and collaborative governance models. People will make the difference.

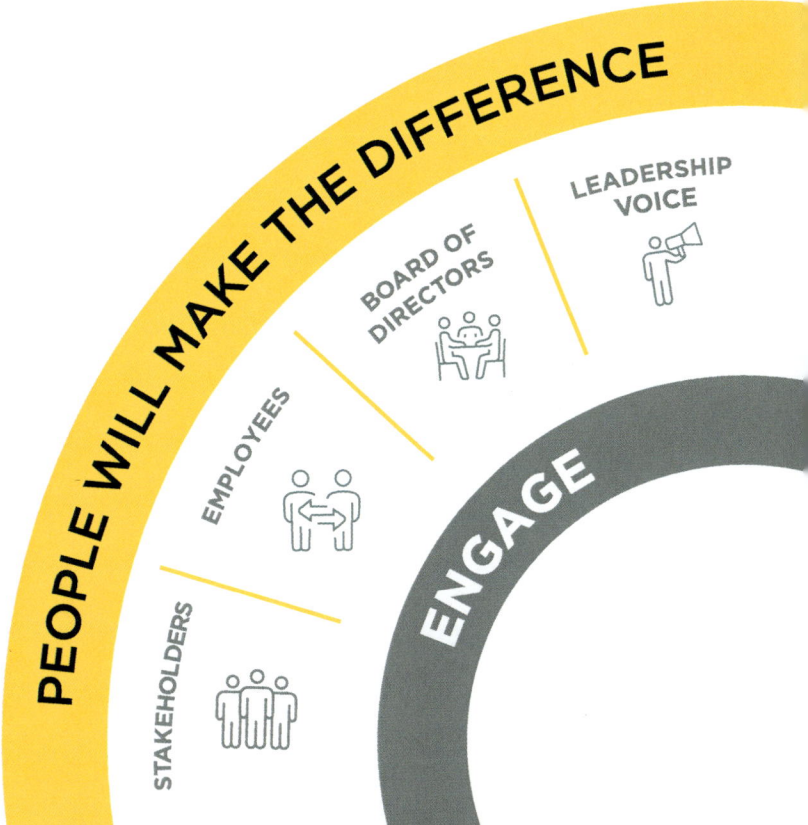

There is a children's rhyme I really like. It tells the story of a little fish who is insignificant alone in a vast ocean, but once joined by hundreds or thousands more the group irresistibly draws even the predators nearby into their current. The business world is somewhat similar — with the distinction that change can only come from within the company itself, and thus through the people who drive these organizations. In other words, while partnership is crucial, to truly have an irresistible force driving towards a new model, the engine driving change must come from the heart of the company and be fueled by all employees and stakeholders.

Again, just as with embodying the vision, we have all grown aware of the importance of creating innovative organizational and decision-making models. But the "how" can still stump us — especially since, in matters of governance, there seems to be, much like seasonal fashion collections, a new theory almost every season. I do not claim to offer any ready-made solution here, as each company has its own culture. However, I can testify to what I have seen, experienced, and evaluated in the companies where I have worked as an employee and advised as a consultant. There indeed are significant trends at play, key principles that outline a new way of making decisions and involving all stakeholders, as well as rallying all employees into a unified movement.

STAKEHOLDERS: KNOWING
YOUR PLAYING FIELD

I n the texts of the three major monotheistic religions, the first time God speaks to humans, He says, "Listen." There is broader truth in this attitude: to act, and to act well, one must first and foremost listen. In business, it's the same. To implement open and authentic governance that allows everyone to be heard, respected, and above all, involved in the model shift, one must first listen to all stakeholders and take their opinions into account.

GET TO KNOW YOUR ECOSYSTEM

But first, who are these famous stakeholders – whom I have already mentioned several times in this book? The term refers to all the actors who participate, directly or indirectly, in the life of the company. Its economic life, certainly, but also its mission, i.e. the objective it has set for itself to advance society and protect nature. While stakeholders have occasionally appeared in a shareholder-driven business model, they have become central in purpose-driven models. It is for and because of these business partners that the purpose is formulated. That's why the new model of purpose-driven companies can be referred to as a partnership model.

Within this category, one can make a distinction between internal — e.g. executives, employees, shareholders, unions — and external stakeholders: suppliers, customers, communities, institutions, NGOs, and civil society. Listening to stakeholders therefore requires willingness, as this category encompasses numerous, diverse groups. ISO 26000 has already laid the foundation for this dialogue between a company and its ecosystem in the context of sustainable development. Here, I must clarify that sustainable development does not only refer to the preservation of the planet, but also to social progress in all its components. While this standard broadly outlines corporate social responsibility, it says little, if anything, about how companies can concretely involve all those who revolve around them.

Finally, consultation can lead to a concrete and co-constructed project, as was the case for Decathlon. Despite the pandemic, the company developed a strategic vision written by tens of thousands, including teammates, employees, clients, and partners. This vision then led to the implementation of a series of action plans to bring this collective dynamic to life.

THE USER MANUAL

There are a few concrete ways to engage stakeholders in a collective process to jointly establish priorities for the coming years. First, openness — reaching out to stakeholders drawing from their perspectives and including their voice. This more inclusive and collaborative approach allows for growth, creating value for each of them in the future, thereby anchoring the company's growth within a global ecosystem. This approach ultimately creates shared progress with the communities in which we operate, as well as the country we live in. It's this very principle that led to the creation of the Business Roundtable on Corporate Governance, which brings together 181 leaders from major American companies annually to "redefine a company's mission together, with the aim of promoting an economic model that serves all Americans." While we haven't formalized an equivalent in France, companies will increasingly have labs and committees — namely, Mission Committees, Stakeholder Committees, or Sustainable Development Councils — which bring together a few employees while also inviting experts to the table.

For instance, Guerlain has taken inspiration from nature for several years. Under Laurent Boillot's leadership, Guerlain has pledged to preserve the planet, and to ensure the quality and longevity of their creations. The company established a Sustainable Board comprising 13 independent experts who were invited to deliberate on the brand's strategic direction, aiming to better reconcile luxury and sustainable development. This innovative committee has been assisting the brand in envisioning new ways to formulate a greener and more sustainable trajectory, especially concerning raw material traceability and the development of fairer and more sustainable supply chains. This new committee also convenes twice a year to assess the company's past actions and realign strategy against new sustainability challenges. As described by Cécile Lochard, Director of Sustainable Development, "with Guerlain's Sustainable Board, we're not seeking mere endorsement of our efforts, but rather an accelerator. Each member has been chosen for their recognized expertise and their freedom to express their convictions." Such leadership allows for this approach to thrive in their new home. Dior Parfum & Hennessy are in great hands!

TRUST AS THE NEW CURRENCY

As we enter an era of multistakeholder capitalism, companies are expected to bring benefits beyond profit. The success of a company to do so relies on two cornerstones: extra financial indicators and trust. Trust is indeed becoming a cardinal value for organizations. Studies from The World Economic Forum have shown that organizations who have trust in their stakeholders perform 5% better than others, and up to 11% better in times of crisis.[24]

Trust refers to the belief or confidence that stakeholders, including customers, employees, investors and partners, and the public, have in a company or organization. It entails the expectation that the company will act with integrity, reliability and honesty in its interactions, commitments and operations. But let's be aware that this dimension is not so straightforward. It goes beyond mere logic, reasoning, and judgment. It also relies on a company's ability to display both authenticity and empathy. Trust will impact your company's reputation among consumers. But trust will also give you to be given the benefit of the doubt.

Make no mistake. Trust is managed from the inside out; it has its ups and downs. But whatever you do, trust remains the ultimate currency in any relationship. It can be monitored and measured as highlighted by Edelman: trusted companies are six times more likely to benefit from consumer loyalty and eight times more resilient.[25]

NEW ROLES IN THE CORPORATE WORLD

The question of corporate culture is at the heart of any model shift. Indeed, any reluctance primarily arises from practices deeply ingrained in our habits, to the point where it's sometimes difficult to distinguish the essential from the accessory. That's why, to infuse this culture with new dynamics, certain companies have explicitly appointed a transformation and stakeholder engagement officer. Thus, for authentic transformation that stems from the heart, it's necessary to envision roles that didn't exist before — bridging the gap between the company's internal and external realities.

However, this endeavor also demands specific talents and particular qualities. These individuals must possess a sense of collectivity, a drive to rally others around a project they believe in, the flexibility to understand diverse individuals and profiles, and a willingness to fully involve those in the company's processes. To formalize and structure this approach — which is also a concrete attitude — many companies are now considering recognizing a distinct role, that of a Stakeholder Officer. This is the choice made by companies like BNP Paribas with Antoine Sire several years ago and La Banque Postale more recently with Adrienne Horel-Pagès, which have established an Engagement Directorate, reporting to the Executive Committee on the progress and outcomes of major consultations with stakeholders.

A life not lived
for others
is not a life.

MOTHER TERESA

Carrefour has also taken this path. I have had the opportunity to work with Alexandre Bompard and his teams, and I have witnessed the emergence of their "Act for Food" program. More than a tagline, it outlines their commitments and concrete actions for promoting food transition. Carrefour started by excluding 100 controversial substances from food supplies, working towards better accessibility of 100% French organic product, and committing to reduce the number of GMOs in the livestock's food intake to 0.9%.26 The program also represents an opportunity for distributors and manufacturers, since they're invited to shift from an exclusively transactional relationship with the company to a more strategic collaboration focused on value creation. Carrefour initiated this several years ago with its suppliers, engaging around ten of them initially to jointly experiment with a path toward healthier and more sustainable food consumption.

Recently, Carrefour teamed up with seven industry partners — Danone, Unilever, Bel, Andros, Bonduelle, Nutrition & Santé, Savencia — to launch a coalition* trying to boost the sales of plant-based alternatives. These companies are aiming to generate three billion in sales from plant-based products by 2026.27 This commitment also extends to the company's internal organization: a portion of each employee's variable remuneration is now linked to the Food Transition Index of their ESG roadmap. The company has even gone further, when Carine Kraus joined the Group Executive Committee, as Executive Director of Engagement.

As for me, I believe that commitment has always been at the heart of my actions. It was the case when I built and led April's international division, a network of entrepreneurs in 36 countries, where I used to say that our motto was 1+1 = 10. In the past decade, I have learned to engage as a catalyst on a larger scale while at Danone, serving the strategic transformation of One Planet One Health — with partners and employees alike. Back in 2014, collaboratively shaping this strategy with colleagues and stakeholders was quite a pioneering choice. There's no magic formula. But one may identify a few ingredients for success: embedding fundamentals at the core of the business model, thinking big even when starting small, rallying others around a vision, genuinely committing, daring to break traditional organizational models, surrounding oneself with the right partners, beginning with the most enthusiastic leaders, drawing from those who are more advanced, shedding light on this path, moving toward new financial mechanisms. Acting together means being ready to go further. It also means being ready to grow, and most importantly to grow together.

These are all signals that will prove the existence of an intention to establish a collective and transparent style of governance, which will transform the model on an organizational scale.

Tony PARKER, Président, Infinity Nine Group and former professional basketball player

We have so much to learn from high-level athletes. Beyond being a basketball legend — considered to be the greatest French basketball player of all time — Tony Parker is also a serial entrepreneur and a dedicated leader, an ambassador for causes centering women and children, and more recently, an education ambassador for the 2024 Olympic Games in Paris last summer. He was one of our first clients at Goodness & Co.

"I have been an advocate for uniting people since my early childhood. I started playing basketball at a young age and had the privilege to realize what a difference the strength of a collective can make. It was by drawing strength and expertise from my teammates, coaches, and opponents that I was able to achieve success in my professional sports career. Since then, it's been one of the pillars of my entrepreneurial life: identifying the uniqueness of each partner, employee, person, and drawing inspiration from them to reach even greater heights. The pioneering spirit that drives me can only be exercised through the spirit of other pioneers, often in fields different from mine, who have managed to define new codes, new rules. That's why I believe in breaking down barriers and creating new, diverse color palettes which our world so desperately needs if we're going to reinvent it. Life is a fantastic playground where unexplored paths are drawn, which we can only tread upon if we've explored the paths taken by the people around us."

STAKEHOLDERS IN ACTION
WHAT IF?

- Who are your stakeholders? This includes both internal stakeholders (employees, leadership, board) and external stakeholders: direct partners (clients, suppliers, employees, NGOs) and stakeholders that impact your organization (governments, institutions, media, competitors, civil society).

- What are your stakeholders' perspectives of your business model? What insights do they provide?

- Is the viewpoint of stakeholders considered in the way you manage the company and make decisions?

- What if you were to create a role of Engagement Director within the Executive Committee?

MOBILIZING
YOUR EMPLOYEES

A study published by McKinsey in 2021 revealed that 70% of employees expect their work to provide them with a sense of purpose.[28] The COVID-19 pandemic has further accelerated this trend, making work not only a place for creating value but also for personal fulfillment. This shift has prompted about two-thirds of individuals surveyed in the same study to reflect on the direction of their life and career during periods of lockdown. With increasing discussions on topics such as "bullshit jobs" (David Graeber, 2018) and "workplace boredom" (*Bore out* by François Bauman, 2016), it's evident that upcoming generations are no longer satisfied with the sole promise of a salary. Nine in ten Gen Zs (86%) and millennials (89%) say having a sense of purpose in their work is very or somewhat important to their overall job satisfaction and well-being, according to a survey by Deloitte.[29] They are worried about the future and want to work for companies that are doing something about it. They want to give their time and skills to companies that have a positive impact on our planet and societies, and which offer hope. Given this context, it's important to devise ways beyond recruitment (where a company's purpose is becoming markedly more influential) to involve, convince, and retain talents over the long term.

EMPOWERMENT IS THE NAME OF THE GAME

In the words of Adam Grant, "leadership is not about pulling people to follow your path, it is about shining enough light for them to find their own routes. Bosses aim to wield power. They issue commands to maintain power. Leaders strive to empower. They delegate authority to unleash potential."

As Coline Rual, our Empowerment Science Director at Goodness & Co would say, "empowerment is a journey of expanding four cognitive states: a sense of individual autonomy (the freedom to act), a sense of meaning-fulness (the reason for acting), a sense of self-efficiency (the capacity to act), and a sense of impact (the power to act). It starts with embodying leadership. It is about motivating and inspiring others through their own actions and behaviors. Structural empowerment refers to empowering conditions at work. It relates to external factors of empowerment, such as participation in decision-making and access to training.

It is not a one-time event or a static state, but a rather dynamic and evolving journey. It goes beyond simply delegating tasks or giving autonomy. It is about fostering a culture that values and encourages employees to take ownership, make decisions and drive positive change in the organization."

Empowering employees is more than just a concept, it is a strategic approach that drives engagement, innovation, creativity, loyalty, produc-tivity, and overall business success.

To foster a truly empowered workforce, organizations must shift from top-down approach to collaborative models. Cultivating a leadership mindset at all levels is paramount. By valuing every voice, as exempli-fied by companies like Danone and KPMG, organizations can create a culture where employees feel heard and valued. Recognizing and rewarding contributions is equally crucial. Beyond individual recognition, these practices play a pivotal role in creating a culture of emulation. By highlighting the successes of colleagues, organizations facilitate vicar-ious experiences: employees observe their peers succeeding and thus strengthen their own belief in their ability to achieve similar outcomes. Empowerment can become a new norm.

BUILDING A TRUST-BASED CULTURE

While employees choose a place to work based on their values and beliefs, trust is also becoming a driver of value creation. Recent research done by Gallup — a meaningful organization which understands the dynamics that drive the future of work — has underlined critical blind spots. Most employees are unsure whether their organizations will always treat customers ethically. Only one-third of employees believe their company is honest and transparent with customers and only one fourth of employees trust their company to do the right thing over immediate profit.[30]

Trust has become more important than ever. Many corporate cultures encourage opportunistic behavior, in a hypercompetitive environment, creating the unfortunate consequence that is ethical blindness. As a result, trusting relationships are harder to sustain. Employees in high-trust organizations are more productive, have more energy at work, collaborate better and stay longer within the company. Trust is a team sport. We need to practice it together, share "the why" behind big decisions, build rituals among team members and dare to have courageous conversations about ethics.

BALANCE AND FULFILLMENT

In the transition to a new business model, I have observed three key elements to cultivating a generation of activists within a company and fostering the loyalty and engagement of all employees. The first pertains to the fundamentals which are sometimes lumped together — often inaccurately — under the broad label of "workplace well-being". The International Labour Organization has delved deeply into this subject. However, after the pandemic, we've come to realize that the new significant health concern is that of mental health. For instance, in the UK, the number of adults experiencing depression doubled post-pandemic, while 40% of young people report stress at work.[31] In this context, issues of well-being cannot be taken lightly as future generations will be the first ones to be affected.

Trust is of paramount importance. This is often referred to as the "Tone at the Top", where the example set from the highest ranks cascades down and ensures the commitment of all, from executive leadership to the most junior roles. Focusing on the overall well-being of each employee will help them align their personal and professional lives, facilitating practices that respect human rights, such as the right to disconnect. Employees with a better work-life balance will be more inclined to stay within the company and become change advocates, as they find opportunities for growth and fulfillment in their roles.

This is what led the co-founder and CEO of Airbnb, Brian Chesky, to recently announce a significant push towards remote work. His employees are now allowed to work from wherever they choose. This flexibility particularly appeals to digital nomads. With these new practices, the company has also devised ways to maintain a sense of community through regular seminars.

SUPPORTING EMPLOYEE INVOLVEMENT

More and more companies are getting all their employees involved in the elaboration of a new chapter in their strategy. In 2005, Leroy Merlin, one of the leading home improvement chains in Europe, made all their employees take part in their "Vision Acceleration" program, through which the company collected their thoughts and ideas to shape its future. During the process, employees expressed their willingness to assist those for whom visiting stores can be challenging, such as disabled and elderly individuals. They offered to come to these customers' homes to help them with product fittings — a service that leverages the expertise of their teams. This is how the Leroy Merlin Corporate Foundation was created in 2006.

The foundation is not intended to replace public structures of support, but rather to provide financial sponsorship in instances where the work could not be carried out without it. What sets this foundation apart is that its existence and survival rely solely on the commitment of its employees. They support families throughout their projects from the administrative

"

TALENT
WINS GAMES,
BUT **TEAMWORK** AND
INTELLIGENCE **WIN**
CHAMPIONSHIPS

"

MICHAEL JORDAN

formalities through to the handover of the work; and the relationship often continues well beyond that point. The foundation's mission is in line with that of the company: "We can build everything together, even the future." In 15 years, 1000 households have been supported by 2500 employees.

MOBILIZING 100% OF YOUR EMPLOYEES

The second crucial factor to efficient employee mobilization lies in the quality of their involvement in decision-making. I am not referring to, of course, a strategy where every single person would be involved in every decision. Rather, companies need to consider seeking input from all employees via platforms for their most significant strategic directions. Small group workshops, as undertaken by Enedis, are also valuable. In my area of expertise, this is what the *Danone One Voice* consultation has sought to achieve. Twice a year, all 100,000 *Danoners are* invited to assess the progress of the company's nine missions and to provide their input on top priority challenges for the group, their team, their business unit, and their country. They can also make recommendations and suggest actions that might accelerate progress. This goes far beyond a mere satisfaction survey.

Marie Guillemot, the President of KPMG's Executive Board, has also provided a great example of commitment to creating responsible value. She places meaning and impact at the core of her growth model. Therefore, upon celebrating the company's 100th anniversary, KPMG's leaders decided to transform it into the first mission-driven consulting firm. Collective mobilization was crucial for achieving this profound transformation. The first step involved rallying the company's 10,000 employees — the firm's primary assets — and helping them become agents of change. Through this exceptional team mobilization and the support of a multidisciplinary team of experts and leaders from various markets, KPMG committed to a new, sustainable, and responsible form of prosperity. Regular interactions with about fifty major economic players provide valuable insights.

Its leadership chose to go further by involving the firm's talents more fully through the creation of a Next Generation Committee; comprised of 13 young members, the committee's role is to regularly challenge the Executive Committee on strategic matters.

Embracing the bylaws of a mission-driven company is the confirmation of this broader cultural transformation. This path of continuous progress requires humility, perseverance, and collective enthusiasm to bridge the gap between words and action.

EMPLOYEE TRAINING

A recent study indicated that eight out of ten young individuals are ready to play their part in transforming business models. This is likely why more and more companies are training their employees in ESG, but there is still a long way to go. It's in every company's interest to train its employees on environmental and societal issues to enable them to become in-house activists. Employee training is essential as it empowers everyone to actively participate in the impact revolution. It is one of the tools for change, offering employees the opportunity to progress and giving them the resources to turn into agents of change. Empowerment is the root of Goodness & Co., and it is the reason why we launched the Goodness Academy. This platform will aim to make sustainability training accessible to everyone within a company, regardless of their role, and inspire each employee to become an agent of change. The backbone of our program will be empowerment, turning each employee into an impact activist. The program delivers the tools necessary to understand the fundamentals about ESG issues, combining insights with best practices. It is about engaging employees and empowering impact optimists.

THE WORLD THROUGH THE EYES OF YOUTH

The media, and sometimes the corporate world itself, have allowed a radical image of Millennials and Generation Z to spread — as demonstrated by the treatment of endeavors such as Great Thunberg's ecological battle or, more recently, the passionate speech delivered by AgroParitech students. They are portrayed as anti-establishment and rejecting the corporate world. I believe they are saying "enough is enough" to the traditional model. These generations are more demanding because they're aware of the collective challenges we are facing, the ones the IPCC has yet again alerted us to in its latest report. Global resource consumption has doubled in the last 30 years. It is imperative that we reinvent our models. If Gen Y and Z expect more from the corporate world than previous generations, it's because they've understood the role which the corporate world plays in responding to the climate crisis. I have much hope in those new generations who refuse to accept inconsistent behavior or tolerate a gap between words and actions.

To attract talent, companies need to consider the demands of younger generations, which goes beyond a search for purpose. It is a calling to be "useful to the world." Signing an employment contract for the mere advantage of getting a paycheck will soon be an outdated practice. Nearly half of young people would be ready to refuse a job offer if a company is not sufficiently committed to ESG issues.[32] When I was a Catalyst for Danone, I was able to witness that the transition to a purpose-led company increased our ranking in the "most attractive employer" list by 20 points among students. Young people prefer companies that are committed to these issues.

Companies must therefore set inner cultural revolutions in motion to include this new generation of activists. This first and foremost means ensuring the fundamentals i.e. their well-being at work. Just a few years ago, this was a non-issue; it has now become a central one. Taking care of employees is becoming a priority, and some companies are no longer hesitating to reinvent how they work, such as Airbnb, which now allows employees to work entirely remotely. Engaging employees means empowering their talents, inspiring, igniting, driving, encouraging, and committing.

THE NEW GENERATION OF SHADOW EXECUTIVE COMMITTEES

Finally, in my view, a practical solution for engaging employees and transforming them into activists is to involve specifically millennials and gen-z more effectively. They are inherently more aware of the urgency to act. Thus, I recommend establishing small volunteer groups to address specific topics, ranging from new collections to environmental engagement within the company.

In this regard, my suggestion would be the setting up of a Next Generation Committee (sometimes referred to as a Shadow Executive Committee). This would be composed of young individuals put in charge of accelerating cultural change and ushering in a new framework for considering positive impact within the company. Modeled after Downing Street's Shadow Cabinets in London, this concept was first implemented and quickly gained traction in the early 2000s by Jack Welch, CEO of General Electric. One benefit of such committees is that young members have not yet been conditioned by hierarchical pressures and are not accustomed to the type of processes which tend to stifle voices and necessary action.

Notable examples of such initiatives include Jo & Joe Brand, a brand developed by and for young people within the Accor group, as well as the Accor Pass, a subscription for those under 25 helping them find temporary accommodation while apartment hunting. These initiatives allowed the group to reinvent itself amid Airbnb's significant pressure on the market. Ardian followed a similar path with their 2017-created Millennial Committee, which is composed of 15 employees under 35 who participate in strategic discussions and regularly provide recommendations to the Executive Committee.

One of the primary benefits of creating a New Generation Committee is also the platform it offers to sometimes unconventional, innovative, and authentic voices. Young members can express themselves freely in a supportive and safe environment. Another significant advantage is the profound impact which formally integrating the Shadow Executive Committee into the organizational structure can have. Doing so not only fosters talent recruitment and retention but also supports the growth and career development of committee members, who are more likely to engage in impact-related matters. These committees recognize the value and expertise of young individuals who march with Greta Thunberg and are highly sensitive to the human and environmental challenges we are facing — migrant crises, widespread poverty, food and water insecurity, and more. With their insights into prevailing trends and actions through new communication channels, they can significantly aid companies align with the world as it stands today. This is the kind of expertise no company should overlook.

CEMENTING THE PARADIGM SHIFT

By initiating such endeavors, I am convinced that new models will be fully operational for the next generation. This is why it is crucial for large corporations to attract those younger individuals, given those companies' enormous potential impact on the world.

To illustrate the tremendous benefit of closely involving the young in a company's major decisions, let's consider the contrasting example of luxury brands Prada and Gucci, whose fashion prowess needs no introduction. Until recently, Prada had been enjoying substantial margins thanks to its legendary creative direction. However, in 2014, sales started declining. According to former co-CEO Patrizio Bertelli, the company was "too slow to recognize the significance of digital channels and web influencers disrupting the sector." This led to an over 11% drop in revenue between 2014 and 2018. Meanwhile, Gucci, under the leadership of Mario Bizzarri, adapted to the market and emerging trends. Through its millennial-headed Shadow Board, the brand kept in tune with societal changes and heeded the advice coming from young talents across various roles. As a result,

Gucci's sales skyrocketed, experiencing a 136% increase in just four years.[33] This is undeniable evidence of the benefits of widening our corporate decision-making bodies.

Recruiting young talents isn't easy. However, when companies realize that showcasing their societal knowledge and impact is vital for attracting candidates, everything becomes possible. According to figures published by the Harvard Business Review, it only takes 10% of employees for a business to change direction and practice.[34] This can motivate a new generation of enthusiastic activists because they know they're participating in something bigger than themselves, in progress. I believe that ideas, people, and actions can change the world. Let's dare to trigger this paradigm shift; let's promise to listen to Millennials, and Generation Z. Let's jointly create our future with them.

Marie GUILLEMOT, Chairwoman of the Board, KPMG France

Being an authentic leader requires aligning words and actions. Marie is one of a kind leader, acting every day with sincerity and determination. Change can help us grow or it can paralyze us. We know what Marie stands for, and she is so eager to move the needle!

"Alone, we can go faster; together, we can go further. Faced with the greatest challenges for the future of humanity and the living world, this African proverb lights the way. I am convinced that collective momentum involving citizens, companies, associations, and public authorities is a necessity to build a more sustainable and responsible economy, a more inclusive and united society.

This profoundly changes how one leads a company. At KPMG, my aim is to provide vision, set a course, and offer teams enough space to co-construct a shared future, teeming with diversity, different perspectives, and a desire to act. Our transformation is based on a commitment pact built on strong, shared values and trust. To sustainably ensure a concerted, intense effort to drive change, we need teams that embrace the vision and values, translating them into everyday actions. I see my role as that of both a guide and a supporter — stimulating, listening, supporting, adjusting, and unleashing energies and audacity. This is what I love and what excites me!

We chose to transform our firm into a mission-driven company to create a path of progress that allows employees to combine professional engagement and personal convictions through a contribution to the common good with impactful results. By addressing their thirst for initiative and action, we can best mobilize our talents. This structured and powerful framework of commitment gives everyone the choice to contribute, alongside their co-workers, according to their desires, to economic, ecological, and social performance. In my view, it's the best way to build a new responsible and sustainable version of prosperity!"

MOBILIZE EMPLOYEES IN ACTION
WHAT IF?

- What motivates your employees to work in your company?

- Do young talents have a say in the company's strategic decisions? Are you willing to listen to them?

- Are you prepared to establish a more collaborative style of governance, not only for specific issues but as a systematic practice, especially when it comes to significant company directions?

- Would you be open to implementing a Next Generation Committee which would challenge the Executive Committee and implement meaningful initiatives?

Reinventing governance
starts with the right board,
composition, and mindset.
But this is not enough,
**it is about embedding
the purpose in every decision**
to ensure sustainable business.

GETTING THE
BOARD ON BOARD

O ver the previous pages, I have shared how new governance models are emerging driven by a partnership approach, the mobilization of new generations, and rise of activists. Additionally, I highlighted the introduction of new roles within large companies that are capable of catalyzing change. However, there remains a central actor I have not yet addressed: the board of directors.

We are entering a new era in terms of governance. The board of directors is critical when it comes to stewardship for sustainable business. The relationship between short-term profit for shareholders and a company's long-term impact on society is a complicated one. 91% of directors think they should dedicate more time to ESG. Yet 70% of Board Members do not feel efficient when integrating sustainability into their business strategies and governance.[35] We are not moving fast nor far enough.

However, the responsibilities of the board of directors should not be solely confined to safeguarding the immediate financial interests of investors; they must also encompass the wellbeing of all stakeholders and society. I recall a particularly acerbic cartoon by the artist Voutch: in a plush boardroom, men with big bellies and two women are holding a meeting. The president stands and says, "For our company, this question raises both an ethical and an economic problem. If nobody objects, let's proceed directly to the economic problem." This cartoon is particularly revealing of the image that society holds of the boards of directors from the last century.

A boards' role must therefore be reexamined to avoid further scandals like the one that hit ExxonMobil in 2018. The multinational oil and gas company was exposed for concealing from its investors the effects of its activities on the climate. An activist hedge fund then compelled the addition of three new members to the board of directors to oversee climate-related matters. Despite this effort, it wasn't enough. In May 2024, ExxonMobil attempted to take legal action against shareholder voices, to block two climate-focused investor groups from introducing a resolution to demand further action to cut Exxon's greenhouse gas emissions. Boards play a crucial role in building new business models for positive change, but without the proper support and accountability, their actions will fall short. This decision shows the importance of protecting shareholder rights without fear of litigation, to prevent the obstruction of shareholder proposals focused on long term benefits for all stakeholders. It's time for corporate boards to exercise their rights freely and prioritize net positive impacts.

THE WIND OF CHANGE

While a vast majority of board members believe that ESG should be integrated into the company's strategy, only one in two directors acknowledge the role the board of directors should play in envisioning and monitoring ESG objectives. Furthermore, 43% consider that their company's Achilles' heel remains its ability to address ESG challenges at its own level.[36] Board members, with their extensive and impressive careers, often come from backgrounds deeply rooted in traditional paradigms. As a result, adapting to and aligning with the evolving expectations of society and the planet can be challenging. Nevertheless, for a company to have an impact, the board of directors must play a pivotal role. In this regard, when faced with a particularly skeptical board member, one should present the competitive advantage that clearly established ESG objectives and purpose represent. As seen, companies that have taken the time and effort to adopt ambitious roadmaps tend to outperform those who have not.

Despite knowing the need to act and address social and environmental issues, many directors admit they don't know where to start. Thus, the study took the time to identify obstacles preventing boards of directors from fully addressing societal issues, leaving them to operational or communications teams to tackle. It seems lack of knowledge and data is one of the main obstacles (46%), as is lack of transparency from management (43%), and motivation (30%). Interestingly, the study also cites the difficulty of translating ideas into action (27%) and the inability to prioritize ESG issues (26%). Yet, the direct involvement of the board appears to significantly impact the success of an organization's ESG ambitions.

A final nuance needs to be added to this assessment. The involvement of governing and administrative bodies appears to vary greatly from one sector to another and directly depends on the significance of ESG issues for the business. While the financial services and pharmaceutical industries seem particularly aware of the importance of clarifying their commitments, several other sectors may not have fully or begun to grasp their significance.

In my opinion, to better involve these bodies in ESG issues, one must begin by linking the variable remuneration of board members to social and environmental performance, thus recognizing the board's immense responsibility in these matters.

MOVING THE NEEDLE

To engage your board of directors in the grand venture of impact business, it appears that each member must first be equipped with the tools and means to become informed about current major subjects. Lack of knowledge and experience truly acts as a bottleneck; ongoing upskilling and training has become essential, now more than ever. This is why I encourage companies to organize meetings between their board of directors and external experts related to the company's activities. Furthermore, the regular integration of ESG-related topics into the agenda of the board of directors sends a strong message that their strategic role is a priority.

At minimum, an annual review with the board of directors on ESG performance allows each member to understand trends, challenges, and difficulties in objective implementation. I have also witnessed sudden interest from boards when shown concrete examples of the link between ESG and growth.

Finally, new models for the board of directors and executive committees within a company must emerge. Among the already existing models, the most traditional one involves shareholder accountability for the success of ESG objectives. Another model, more prevalent in North America, entails appointing a dedicated ESG committee within the board, whereas in Europe boards traditionally have a single individual responsible for the achievement of ESG goals. ESG committees have become increasingly common and new models are waiting to be developed.

EMBRACE DIVERSITY

Welcoming diversity is a must. Analysis of the Russel 3000 shows women hold just 30% of seats, with little progress in the past years.[37] Historically, companies have recruited directors who are experienced in the context of yesterday's business landscape. In the S&P 500, the average age of a board member is 63.5 years.[38] These leaders may be more comfortable with a passive sustainability strategy of compliance than with challenging business models as a reaction to sustainability challenges.

46% of directors say they are concerned about lack of diversity and points of view within the board.[39] What if the board welcomed directors with different perspectives on business as a force for good, who can deal with complexity, and a wider range of stakeholder perspectives? Bringing together diverse skill sets, areas of expertise, and cultural backgrounds enhances the depth and range of perspectives, leading to more sustainable decision-making. Nature cannot speak on her own, so we must actively speak on its behalf. Composition is critical — achieving racial and gender parity, fostering curiosity, and embracing the right mindset for new ways of doing business.

It all begins with who sits at the table; the composition and diversity of the board are crucial. Since citizens aren't living in your office, it's essential to be curious, upskill yourself, and engage with stakeholders beyond just shareholders. Embracing sustainability means integrating it into the core of your strategy, turning it from a regulatory necessity into a key driver of long-term value. Now is the time to walk the talk by aligning words with actions. Real progress will only come from courageous leaders.

As we enter a new era of governance and leadership, let this gathering be a catalyst for board members and leaders to fully embrace their role as architects of change.

FROM COMPLIANCE TO COMPETITIVITY

This is a business imperative. I believe that in the future, only organizations with a positive impact will thrive, as employees, consumers, partners, and investors will choose to spend their time and money elsewhere. It has now become an issue of competitiveness. Companies with ESG strategies perform better by 13%.[40] The board must be encouraged to spend less time on compliance and sustainability hygiene and more on turning sustainability into a competitive advantage. Spending time on challenging questions is a necessity, to guide the responsibility of the company with all stakeholders, for their suppliers and their employees. We must ask the right questions: how can we make our business model sustainable within the planet boundaries? How can we evolve our product portfolio to better serve the people and our planet? How do we create meaningful value for our consumers? How can we offer sustainability-related propositions that will be valued by customers? How can we accelerate this shift and have a greater impact?

At the time of urgency, we need to transform the board of directors into true catalysts of change. Shifting from a regulatory compliance logic to a value creation logic starts with directors acting as Change Makers. This is why we set up a specific Board members program at ChangeNOW, with the amazing co-founder Kevin Tayebaly and partners such as Kering, INSEAD and IFA. Our aim is to instill new practices within the Boards of Directors so they can fully take on their essential role in building sustainable futures. Less than 14% of CEOs can perform and transform at the same time, while 40% of sustainability initiatives are due to investor pressure, according to SSRN. All agree about the critical value Boards do play when it comes to stewardship for sustainability in business, yet more than half agree that they need to do it more effectively. What is holding the Boards back from taking responsibility on sustainability issues? What role should the Board play in the transformation? How can this body actively reconcile business and ESG performance? Addressing these topics together in the Chatham House rule encourages an open dialogue and creates a trusted environment for everyone to progress.

KEEPING EVERYONE ACCOUNTABLE

It is no longer an activist issue; it is everyone's business. Progress has been made. A new wave of stricter extra-financial regulation is coming. The CSRD encompasses 50,000 European companies which had not yet been targeted so far. All companies with over 250 employees, 40 million euros in turnover or 20 million euros in net profits will have to publish detailed reviews about their extra-financial performance. Those companies are being pushed towards greater transparency to avoid greenwashing.

Likewise, an increasing number of boards have a CSR committee — from 25% in 2015 to 61% in 2021 in the top 120 largest French companies.[41] A shift is happening, but we are still lacking the tools to entirely make the case for the connection existing between performance and positive impact. We are facing a system with too few incentives. So, what if we aligned directors' remuneration based on their company's ESG performance? Whatever the method, we must realign the objectives with a sense of reward or sanction.

I believe time has come. Conscious leaders are becoming more of a movement than a niche, and investors are catching up to speed as well. We have 10 years. 10 years to embrace the entrepreneurial spirit at board level to reinvent the way we do business.

REINVENTING CORPORATE GOVERNANCE TO PROTECT THE COMPANY'S MISSION

Some companies decided to secure the longevity of their mission and strategy by adjusting their legal structure and governance bodies. The most recent example on everyone's lips is Patagonia. In 2022, founder Yvon Chouinard and his close family decided to hand their shares and voting rights over to a trust. This was decided to make sure that the operations of the company would stay in line with its values and mission. Such a move remains unique on the market, especially when it comes to its estimated value of 3 billion dollars and ensuing legal structure.

In France, Naos, known for its skincare brands Bioderma and Esthederm, implemented in 2018 a specific governance model designed by its founder, Jean-Noël Thorel. In 2011, Thoel wrote what he called a constitution for the company, summarizing its core values and business priorities. To ensure the sustainability of the company's model and goals, ownership and voting rights have been intentionally separated. Pierre Fabre operates under a similar model, with a specific legal structure in place. Since the death of its founder, a foundation has owned the majority of the company.

Denis TERRIEN, Chairman, IFA (the French Institute of Directors)

Several years ago, Denis realized that board rooms are playing a pivotal role in this transformation. Board members are concentrating on sustainable business practices and the mid to long-term performance of the company, while the executive team is more focused on short-term results. Conscious about the role of governance, Denis encouraged the shift to happen.

"When one looks at a range of companies, one thing is certain: there is not one unique winning formula. I've learned that companies which align vision and action and are led by men and women with shared values, usually succeed. The thing which brings together vision, values and action is called governance.

The board of directors is at the center of governance. It is the place where major decisions are made such as naming a new CEO and deciding how that person will be rewarded, approving strategy and the yearly budget, helping the CEO manage risks, and communicating to markets. Other major decisions such as deciding on the company's purpose, large acquisitions, and divestitures, are also debated and decided on by the board of directors.

Historically, governance has always been more focused on producing financial returns for its shareholders. The last 20 years have seen it evolve with an increased demand for it to ensure a fair distribution of value amongst stakeholders and to improve its impact on the environment and society in general. Moreover, as the world has become more complex and new regulations have been put in place, the board members' responsibilities have increased. Hence, the most efficient boards ensure diversity in skills, talents and gender while promoting collegiality and exchanges between directors; this is necessary to create collective intelligence in the service of better decision making and to anticipate uncertainties and doubts.

My 20-year-old experience sitting on boards has taught me that good governance usually leads to success whereas bad governance always leads to failure. One is not born a good board member. One becomes one. Hence, I call upon all future board members to get proper, serious training and to have the courage to make responsible decisions in order to create lasting value."

THE BOARD IN ACTION
WHAT IF?

- What if Boards of Directors were gender balanced, fostered curiosity, and embraced the right mindset for new ways of doing business for sustainable futures.

- What if Board of Directors dedicated time for strategic questions related to the ESG strategy, the value creation of the company for all stakeholders, and the actions needed?

- What if all Directors underwent ESG training?

- What if Boards systematically considered ESG in its investment decisions, strategy development, and innovation review?

I have learned that you are never **TOO SMALL** to make a **DIFFERENCE**.

GRETA THUNBERG

LEADERSHIP
VOICE

American sociologist John Austin can be credited with reviving the idea that there is power in the mere declaration of an ambition. To state something is already to commit to action. It's the first step of acting. Simply put, when a company announces a change, a courageous decision — for example, to eliminate plastic packaging by 2025 — it binds itself, in a certain way, to follow through if it wants to maintain the trust of its customers and its entire ecosystem.

The voice of a company also lies in its ability to move boundaries, such as regulations, to collectively rethink tomorrow's economic paradigms. It's undeniable that the voice of a collective is stronger than that of an individual actor — this is the very principle of public affairs and professional associations. This cannot be accomplished without bringing the company's voice closer to that of its leadership.

EMBODYING CHANGE

During her mandate as Prime Minister of New Zealand, Jacinda Arden demonstrated something new: leaders can be anxious, sensitive, kind and wear their heart on their sleeve. Arden wanted climate change to be front and center of her administration and she made it so in a truly inspirational way.

Treatises on leadership proliferate in bookstores like daffodils in spring. Not a day goes by without erudite professors of even ancient history

WE ALL HAVE
THE **POWER
TO AWAKEN**
THE CONSCIENCE
OF **THE WORLD**.

producing their own theories of leadership — drawing parallels between Julius Caesar and Boris Johnson or a prince of Syracuse and our current president. However, there is an aspect of leadership which, to me, remains inadequately addressed. It is the influence of companies themselves – not just their leaders — on society. In other words, all companies have something relevant to say to society about their fields of expertise. This means that they must be able to work on and express their opinions on these subjects, developing communication in an accessible language while daring to debate with academics and political figures.

Therefore, the social role of a company also lies in its ability to intervene on subjects that matter to them, as identified by their ecosystem, without fear of being too politicized or losing customers who might disagree. Often seen from a communication perspective, the company's voice, in my view, must also be integrated into the question of its impact on society. It's also, of course, a means to unite employees and stakeholders, to participate in debates of ideas and their country's democratic life, and to present your actions for the common good in a different light. Beyond the right to take a stand, it has now become a duty.

EMBRACING SOCIAL LEADERSHIP

A purpose-driven company is not confined to its primary business domain; indeed, it can make impactful statements far beyond its core operations. For instance, Ben & Jerry's, a globally recognized ice cream brand, took an extraordinary step by engaging in the French presidential election campaign and addressing French immigration policies. While this move might seem distant from their usual product focus, it highlights the brand's commitment to broader societal issues. This bold initiative not only drew significant attention to the company but also sparked a meaningful debate through an extensive customer outreach campaign.

Conversely, one would expect companies' opinion when it comes to their activities. The Etam Group undoubtedly has something to say about women's health and issues of self-esteem, Maisons du Monde about deforestation, Natura & Co about biodiversity. As for the Essity Group and its Nana sanitary pad brand, it was among the first industrial actors to draw attention from public authorities to menstrual precarity. It's helped opening a discussion about reducing the current 5.5% VAT on feminine hygiene products.

A VOICE THAT'S WORTH SO MUCH MORE

Since the CEO is often the main face of the company, the way a company takes its place in society also depends on its leader's posture. It is the CEO who embodies the alignment of the company between what is being said and what is being done. Through their speeches and participation in conferences, media engagements, symposiums, forums, seminars, and debates — whether at foundations like the World Economic Forum, Annual Summit in Davos or at Change Now, or during summer university courses on the economy of the future — they address topics that matter not only to them personally but also to the companies they represent. Indeed, these priorities will have been chosen collectively, with stakeholders and company employees, within the framework outlined earlier. As a conscious leader, Pascal Demurger, CEO of MAIF wrote a book "The 21st Century Company will be political or will disappear". The world is concerned by too many systemic crisis for its leaders to look away. Pascal went even further as Co-Chair of IMPACT FRANCE, inviting leaders to reinvent the economy, an economy embracing environmental and social progress, and to make it the norm. The modern leader faces a triple imperative — strategic, social, and moral — that implies assuming a new form of leadership, making engagement the very source of collective success. Engagement is first and foremost a strategic imperative.

Marie-Claire DAVEU, Chief Sustainability and Institutionnal Affairs Officer, Kering

The world needs role models. Marie Claire is such a driving force when it comes to business as a force for good. Yes, the bar is high, but we need people setting and achieving ambitious goals. She is someone many of us look up to, demonstrating that it is possible.

"True leadership is about charting new paths and embracing the unknown. I believe that it's a balance between being innovative yet also pragmatic so that one can quickly pivot and change direction when required. Above all, a willingness and the development of optimism are essential, especially when it comes to sustainability. This is part of my leadership philosophy with my team at Kering and we put it into practice daily with our colleagues across our Houses.

Our vision for change is far-reaching at Kering. We believe that the luxury sector can and must break away from tradition, embracing radical strategies for sustainability and using its influence to inspire change. Transforming our business model and re-inventing luxury has been a mission at Kering for fifteen years, decided by our Chairman and CEO, François-Henri PINAULT. We took a pioneering role in sustainability to implement new solutions and technologies. As such, our Environmental Profit and Loss (EP&L) was a ground-breaking tool for both corporate transparency and natural capital accounting. It makes the invisible visible, measuring a company's environmental impacts across the value chain starting from raw material production. In turn, better informed decisions can be made and impact reduction efforts become more effective in driving change.

Through this science-driven approach and key performance indicators decided every year by our CEO, my team has been developing robust policies and our annual EP&L analysis informs our raw material sourcing strategy, manufacturing processes and best-adapted technologies. Innovation also plays a crucial role in reaching our reduction targets, which led us to set up the Kering Material Innovation Lab back in 2013 with a current library of 8,000 sustainable materials.

Creating new solutions is at the heart of our entrepreneurial outlook when it comes to sustainability. It is also why we believe in open-sourcing them for our industry. Leadership in my view is also about collaborative action: that is why the Fashion Pact initiative we established became a world-wide success."

LEADERSHIP VOICES IN ACTION
WHAT IF?

- On what topics would it be legitimate for your company to take a stand?

- How have you committed as a leader? Have you participated in discussions during key forums or published writings on these topics for instance?

- To what extent are you willing, regardless of your role in society, to advocate for these positions, to become a force for proposals on specific issues?

- Would you be willing to participate in drafting a white paper, opinion pieces, or open letters to elected officials?

3.
ACT TO MAKE THE SHIFT HAPPEN!

Turn words into actions

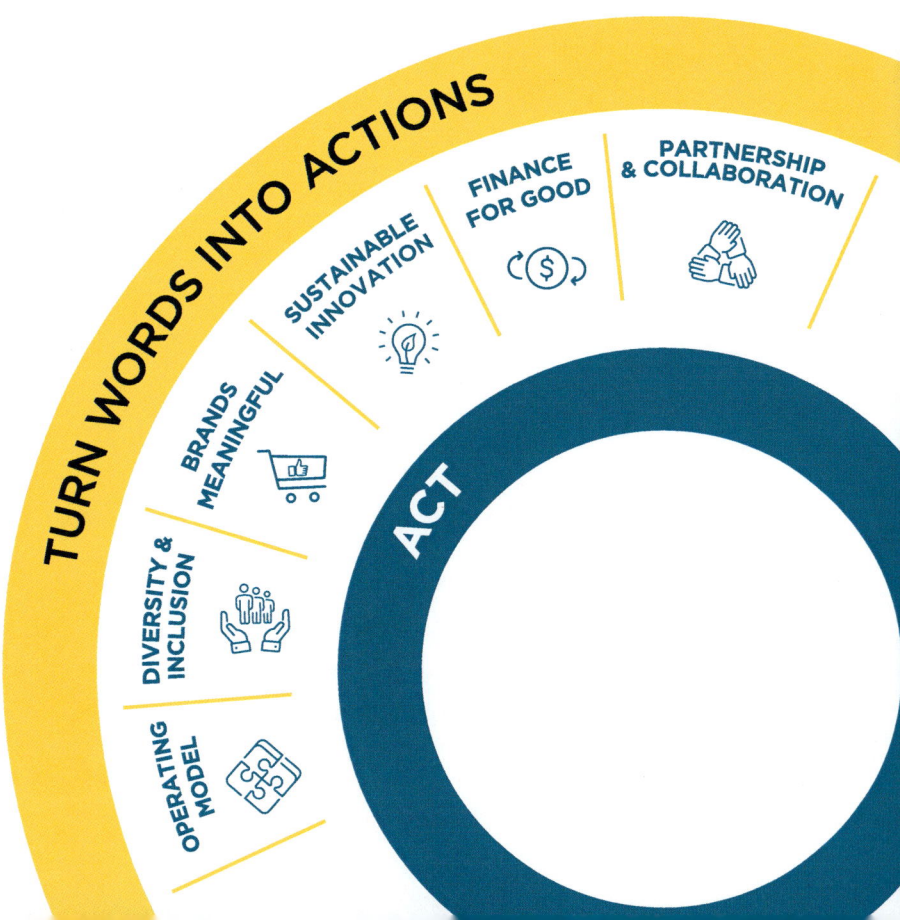

TURN WORDS INTO ACTIONS

ACT

SUSTAINABLE INNOVATION

FINANCE FOR GOOD

PARTNERSHIP & COLLABORATION

BRANDS MEANINGFUL

DIVERSITY & INCLUSION

OPERATING MODEL

Leonardo da Vinci's Mona Lisa's captivating aura lies within the strange power of her look: wherever you are in the room, her eyes will follow you. A somewhat similar pattern is at play in business, especially when discussing ESG issues. Everyone can feel the urgent need to change our approach. Everyone agrees on the need to change management practices or business processes. Yet, when it comes to defining a roadmap and transitioning from words to action, everything seems less straightforward. Like that look that mysteriously follows you, but that you struggle to identify, that you don't know much about.

Indeed, when it comes to ESG objectives, until they are translated into quantifiable goals, they hover over the company without much substance beyond a vague "presence." But where to start? With more collaborative management, eliminating plastic bottles in the offices, industry coalitions to pool resources, or the undertaking of responsible sourcing? Should one duplicate best practices from large corporations when leading a small business, and vice versa? Is it relevant for a member of a bank's board of directors to take inspiration from creative companies in consumer goods?

Each company undeniably has its unique footprint based on its specific products, services, culture, and defined expectations with its employees, suppliers, and clients. But, most importantly, it must be understood that changing models and becoming a purpose-driven company is not a monolithic process. It's a journey, not a fixed destination. A transformation that involves giving more than you'll receive. Thus, the levers I'm about to detail can be activated independently of each other, at the right time, depending on the company's size and core business. Because it's always a bundle of initiatives that gradually shift a conventional organization towards one that makes an impact.

Like a snowball growing as it rolls downhill, accumulating more snow, positive impact is not born out of a magic formula; transforming an organization cannot happen overnight. Instead, it's about trial and error, innovation, course correction, and persistence. One of the few conditions is to keep moving forward and learning while remaining convinced that success is achievable. And every individual, within their team and scope, can make a difference.

The world needs **DREAMERS**, the world needs doers, but above all, the world needs dreamers **WHO DO**.

SARAH BAN BREATHNACH

With great power comes great responsibility.

VOLTAIRE

DEVELOPING A NEW
OPERATING MODEL

What would Megan Rapinoe, the Ballon d'Or winner and FIFA's Best Women's Player, one of our esteemed clients, be without the team she won the 2019 Women's World Cup with? Every teammate had to commit in unison and offer their support. Similarly, conviction and hope alone would not have been enough for Didier Deschamps to make the French team into the champions of the 2018 World Cup. In a business context, things are quite similar. The CEO might fervently hope for the company to become virtuous and contribute to a better world. Workers might seek to create a production line that generates less waste and take actions within their capacities to bring about change. Salespeople might negotiate particularly favorable agreements for ethically produced products. Sourcing departments might make more responsible choices avoiding underpaid or child labor. Marketing could align brands with the causes they stand for and eliminate plastic promotional items. But it's only as a team that they will succeed and turn their company into a platform of progress.

PRINCIPLES-BASED ACTION

Each initiative, at any level, has its importance. However, if those initiatives aren't coordinated and scaled up, their impact remains limited. It's necessary to win the heart of the company and make it beat to a new rhythm. For this, certain overarching principles will foster trust and cooperation among employees, stakeholders, decision-makers, and ultimately society at large. Beyond a corporate climate, it's a genuine internal disposition which facilitates the profound transformation of an organizational culture.

It seems to me, therefore, that the birth of a new model relies on an organizational concept called the principle of subsidiarity. This means that change is everyone's responsibility, and everyone should have the opportunity to act at their level to tackle the issues defined by the company's purpose. This notion also implies collaboration towards the common good within a project that unites and encourages sharing initiatives, discoveries, and progress observed within teams or business units. By fostering creativity and empowering lower levels with decision-making authority, managers can create an environment that supports the development of a new model within the company.

Another key is what I would call the principle of animation. What does this mean? Imagine a living organism. In this organism, the breath – *anima* in Latin — supplies each organ with oxygen, allowing the body to live, move, and act. But *anima* can also mean soul. I like to think of a company's mission, its purpose, as its soul. It's what should animate this vast, sometimes slightly ailing, body that is the company. Another metaphor I use is that of the backbone, which emphasizes that the purpose and ESG objectives cannot be a mere afterthought, detached from the company and being added like a bonus. This distinction is crucial for understanding the difference between genuine impact and actions that are misaligned with the company's purpose, such as greenwashing or social washing. My first two recommendations for sustainably transforming a company are as follows: first, involve everyone. Make this a collective journey across all departments and jointly decide on major directions. This is what's known as the principle of subsidiarity, which is crucial to a model of management which both empowers and trusts its employees. My second recommendation is to integrate impact into the core of the model, letting it drive decisions and give purpose to all company endeavors. However, if one doesn't make the effort of placing social and environmental objectives at the heart of their system or tries to force teams to change their approach without involving them in building the new one, there's a risk that a new model will never sustain long term.

EYES ON THE COMPASS

It's probably not a coincidence that Mars chose Barry Parkin, a sailing enthusiast, as their Chief Procurement & Sustainability Officer. Accustomed as he is to keeping a close eye on navigation data at sea, he likely drew from this habit the courage to craft a compass for his company. Like sailors setting sail, this was a team effort, made in close collaboration with the family members involved in the multinational family business.

When I met the management team at the launch of the Livelihoods Funds — dedicated to biodiversity and food security — I quickly saw that their purpose was not just a passive aspiration, but a sincere and ambitious commitment shared by all their partners.

They were aiming to build a more sustainable world, believing that "the world we want for tomorrow starts with how we do business today." Like an explorer's compass, Mars' compass has four cardinal points: robust financial performance to have the freedom to contribute to a better world; responsible growth of targeted products and services; positive societal engagement for people, their pets, and the planet through a Sustainable in a Generation Plan; trust-based partnerships with all stakeholders.

This is why, at Mars, performance evaluations do not only scrutinize financial performance but also human, environmental, and social components, which are measured against the company's set goals — both in the annual report and in its investments. For the top 300 management individuals, their variable compensation is dependent on the achievement of the objectives outlined by the compass.

When it comes to strategizing change, we must also consider the power of a specific context to strongly encourage a change in direction. I recall a vignette in *Forbes* which asked, "Who led the digital transformation of your company? Answer A: the CEO; Answer B: the CTO." Then, the correct answer: COVID-19![42] What I take from this seemingly casual joke is that the strategic role of leaders also involves adapting to circumstances to help their company progress.

EACH IS RESPONSIBLE FOR ALL

Make no mistake. Transformation at the speed and scale we need is a challenge — especially in markets with many short-term economic and political headwinds. It will not happen overnight. Recent CDP analysis highlights the trials we are facing: out of 18,600 companies with a climate transition plan, only 0,4% were cutting the mustard.[43]

To bring a purpose-oriented strategy to life, I believe it's necessary to rethink the role of the Chief Strategy Officer and transform it into a Chief Impact Officer (CIO). Let me explain. Nowadays, a company's strategy must be explicitly directed towards achieving not only economic but also environmental, social, and societal objectives. Given the pressure from media, investors, stakeholders, regulatory constraints, and demands from customers and employees, it's inconceivable not to place ESG objectives at the heart of the strategy.

Naturally, it seems that the role of a strategist should also encompass overseeing the positive impact of the company on the world. The position of CIO often exists and reports directly to the CEO. This role is undergoing a rapid and dramatic transformation. Historically, CSOs acted like communication executives; their primary task was to create appealing feel-good storytelling. Today, their role is to ensure the actual integration of ESG into corporate strategy — i.e. sustainable value creation. The challenge is about what not to do. Not so easy, I must say. Other companies call this role the Chief Translation Officer, or Catalyst, emphasizing their role as educators, unifiers, and their capacity to rally the corporate environment around a more sustainable and resilient culture at all levels of the company.

ALIGNING INCENTIVES WITH ESG TARGETS

Aligning incentives with ESG targets is not about good ethics, it is about good business. The battle for linking CEO remuneration to the achievement of climate goals was waged by Pascal Canfin, a Member of the European Parliament and Chair of the Environment Committee of the European Parliament, along with about twenty business leaders — including Antoine Frérot (Véolia), Catherine Mac Gregor (Engie) — and investors like Philippe Zaouti (Mirova). Together, they signed a letter urging the European Commission in January 2022 to integrate ESG performance in CEO remuneration. Great progress has been made since: a PWC study published in 2023 concluded that over three-quarters of large businesses have now linked executive pay outcomes to climate targets, as opposed to less than 50% in 2020.[44]

POSITIVE IMPACT IS EVERYONE'S JOB

The appointment of someone to a role specifically responsible for strategy, audits, ESG objective monitoring, and fostering relationships with employees and stakeholders — in essence, having an "impact Swiss Army knife" — can never replace collective commitment in a partnership approach. Therefore, human resources departments must also be involved, particularly when it comes to developing new abilities. Finance plays a pivotal role in the transformation of the decision-making process and ESG reporting. Marketing can also be a powerful lever as it is the department which can conceptualize how brands may act as a force for good and demonstrate their use to society. Procurement can help by revisiting the supply chain. Commercial and sales departments enable you to engage with your clients and to drive competitiveness. Research and Development encourage your innovation to be sustainable by design. Communication roles devise the leadership voice and the commitment of stakeholders.

Each role has their part to play in the impact initiative. As for directors, the executive team, and board members, their remuneration should be particularly linked to ESG performance. But this sort of incentive can absolutely be extended to other employees, as a tangible testament to everyone's responsibility in the success of the paradigm shift. In this regard, I recall a quote from Antoine de Saint-Exupéry — I'm from Lyon, some things never change — which goes: "To be a man is precisely to be responsible. It is to feel, while laying one's stone, that one contributes to building the world." Further on, in *Flight to Arras* (1942), he adds: "Each is responsible for all."[45] I believe this is true, even more so in a for-good company, where everyone is invited to contribute their share. This responsibility is also reliant on the empowerment of each employee, through training and their active involvement in the company's strategic choices.

Cécile BELIOT, CEO, Group Bel

I met Cécile a few years ago when we worked together to launch One Planet One Health at Danone. I particularly admire her leadership and her ability to align her personal and professional aspirations. She commits for real, displaying courage deeply rooted in action. This is indeed the primary quality of those who drive progress.

"To build a more virtuous and sustainable model, faced with economic, social, and climate urgencies, the real question is 'how?' The answer is by placing ESG at the heart of our performance, on the same level as profitability. At Bel, this means making both dimensions the compass and filter for everyone's actions, everywhere, for every decision, whether it's about investments, innovations, or choices in our brand portfolio."

OPERATING MODEL IN ACTION
WHAT IF?

- To what degree are your ESG commitments guiding your strategic decisions, investments, and innovations?

- Is ESG integrated into the incentives scheme of the executive team?

- What role does each function play within the company in achieving ESG objectives?

DIVERSITY, EQUITY,
INCLUSION & BELONGING

The question of *Diversity, Equity, Inclusion and Belonging** (DEIB) is particularly close to my heart. Mirroring the complexities of today's society, DEIB can be understood and reflected upon from six different perspectives: balancing gender representation in businesses, reducing the gender pay gap, favoring equal career development paths, facilitating equal job opportunities, promoting inclusive accessibility for people with disabilities, and fostering multicultural environments for people to thrive.

I witness daily that we are still far from an inclusive model, even when only looking at gender parity in the workplace. However, it took me some time to realize how significantly male-dominated the corporate world could be. It wasn't until I joined Danone, which had very few women in leadership positions at the time, that I became aware of this issue. I also discovered that some male colleagues in equivalent roles to mine were earning salaries 30% higher than my own.

Another wakeup call was during my involvement with the Consumer Goods Forum, where I became aware of the lack of women in top positions within this industry. At that time, there were only ten female CEOs out of 400 companies, even though 75% of products were purchased by women! When Indra Nooyi, the former CEO of Pepsico – a remarkable leader – left the board of the commission I co-chaired in 2018, there were 58 men out of... 58 members! This was the turning point that pushed me to join the International Women's Forum and become the vice president of my region's local branch.

In recent years, I have also come to realize the importance of sisterhood. As I have grown older, I have recognized its power. While, at the beginning of my career, I initially surrounded myself with primarily male mentors, I am now mainly advised and inspired by women. My clients, friends, partners, members of the International Women's Forum, and many others demonstrate the strength of female mutual support, characterized by kindness and generosity. Among women in leadership roles, I have found a unique alignment between the mind, heart, and body.

SETTING OBJECTIVES

In 2023, the gender pay gap had been reduced by 68.6% according to the World Economic Forum, but there is still a long way to go.[46] On average across OECD countries, women earn 11.6% less than men.[47] At this current rate, it will take 132 years to reach perfect parity.[48] Some countries are making progress such as Finland, Norway, Sweden or New Zealand; but the business world still struggles to acknowledge the lack of female talent in companies. Women earn 17% less than men for equivalent positions.[49] In executive committees, there are still four times more men than women.[50] Moreover, women run 10% of Fortune 500 companies while only three of the largest 40 French companies are run by female CEOs — Engie, Orange, and Veolia.[51][52]

Discrimination often begins at the hiring stage. This is the conclusion drawn by a study from the SISTA collective, whose communication campaign left an impact by asking the question, "What if we asked men the same questions as women?" The campaign featured surprising videos in which individuals — for instance, Xavier Niel, founder of Illiad and French billionaire — were asked such questions as if they'd succeeded "thanks to [their] appearance".[53] It's questions like these which are unfortunately commonly directed at women and very rarely at men.

As leaders, we must be champions of diversity and inclusion. It's our **RESPONSIBILITY** to ensure that our organizations are not just diverse, but also inclusive, where **EVERYONE'S VOICE IS HEARD AND VALUED**. This is key to maintaining a competitive edge.

LEENA NAIR

While female talent might not be fully recognized yet, regulatory constraints can help. Following the Copé-Zimmerman laws, the business world discovered that quotas could lead to the emergence of a new generation of female leaders. This supports Mrs. Zimmerman's view that, "When we legislate, we find women. When we don't legislate, we find excuses." In a time when gender parity in the workplace is regressing due to the COVID-19 crisis, I believe that measurable goals can lead to more women being hired for key positions. The direct effects of the Copé-Zimmerman law are evident: within the boards of companies required to adhere (SBF 120), there are now 45% women, compared to less than a quarter in other companies.[54] The EU legislation finally made progress in 2023 by requiring listed companies in all member states to have women take up at least 40% of non-executive board seats by mid-2026.[55]

Why is this a problem? Beyond equity considerations, statistics prove that parity drives innovation, competitiveness, and economic and social performance. Companies are depriving themselves of profits by not promoting female talent. Organizations with gender-diverse executive teams are 21% more likely to experience above-average profitability.[56] Female leadership also contributes to modernizing corporate culture and retaining talent. The deeper reasons for this advantage remain somewhat mysterious, but diversity in all its forms is a source of enrichment and sharing. As Ursula Von der Leyen, the European Commission President said in 2023, "diversity is not a matter of fairness. It also drives growth and innovation. The business case for having more women in leadership is clear."

To measure the feminization of companies, I recommend setting measurable objectives to track the company's progress year after year. Indicators should also be established by function to avoid perpetuating anomalies, such as the fact that 43% of HR directors are women, compared to only 17% of sales directors in France.[57] Therefore, I believe that inclusion will only come through ambitious and measurable objectives, such as eliminating the gender pay gap and achieving a workforce that's 50% female in the long run. On this note, L'Oréal stands out as a pioneer in Diversity, Equity and Inclusion. In 2022, there is no longer a salary gap between women and men in the company, and L'Oréal scored 97/100 on the 2022 Gender Equality Index, making it the highest-rated French company in this regard.[58] This achievement is the result of a generation of leaders who worked hard to create a profoundly egalitarian corporate culture.

EMPOWERMENT AND SUPPORT

I consider it a public interest mission to help young girls aim for the stars. They should dare to pursue leadership positions and overcome the self-doubt that they often subconsciously experience — commonly referred to as the "confidence gap"— repairing women's often warped self-image. This gap can affect anyone regardless of gender.

Building on the legacy of its female founder, Veuve Cliquot was a pioneering player in the promotion of female entrepreneurship. Indeed, the company launched the Bold Woman Award in 1972! As its CEO Jean-Marc Gallot would highlight, "female entrepreneurship is all about audacity, inspiration and determination." Their award supports women on this journey and brings together female entrepreneurs across the globe.

In another sector, LDLC Asvel Féminin, a professional basketball club, has made it their mission to address the problem of women's self-image. This high-level sports club became the first one to adopt the bylaws of a mission-driven company to promote the empowerment of women in all aspects of life. The founders, Tony Parker and Marie-Sophie Obama are on a bold mission. I believe that a passion for sports can be put in the service of societal goals; unlocking potential within any woman through sport, it can create lasting transformations in society. ASVEL has become a symbol of female empowerment, helping each girl and woman achieve their full potential. The club's passion is dedicated to a major social cause, ensuring that every individual can realize their dreams and truly become the "captain of their own life." Their commitment is reflected in initiatives that combat stereotypes and celebrate differences, aiming to prevent shattered dreams and repressed ambitions.

Alexis Perakis, CEO of L'Oréal's Consumer Products Division, shares a similar ambition. He strives every day to create "beauty that moves the world" and leverages his organization for impact. For L'Oréal, beauty shouldn't be limited to appearances but should help every individual gain the confidence to spread their wings and engage with others. It's staggering to realize that this drive to democratize the best of beauty is already impacting over a billion consumers. The "Stand Up" program is one such example that shows how an exceptional group of leaders can make a significant impact. More than a third of women worldwide have experienced physical and sexual violence at least once in their lives, including in the workplace.[59] While the #MeToo movement has significantly raised awareness about these issues, it has not yet fully addressed the deeper, underlying challenges that affect self-perception and confidence. L'Oréal Paris is leveraging its marketing influence to support this cause through comprehensive awareness campaigns and targeted training. Its partnership with the NGO Right To Be has already trained more than 1.3 million people in 41 countries.[60]

I have the pleasure of regularly collaborating with Nathalie Gerschtein, President of L'Oréal North America's Consumer Products Division. Her perspective on life as a woman leader keeps nourishing me. Throughout her career, she's never said no to a new challenge as staying within the status quo rarely leads anywhere, and, because what fundamentally matters is to keep learning. But there is one comment she keeps hearing: "You're too ambitious." Many women with non-traditional paths have frequently heard this comment. Nathalie recalls a TedTalk given by Reshma Suajani, founder of Girls Who Code, which left a profound impact on her when Suajani said, "we teach our girls to be perfect, and we teach our boys to be brave. Nathalie believes it's time for this mindset to change, to bridge this ambition gap. We need to redefine what it means to dare, take risks, and

DIVERSITY is being invited to the party; **INCLUSION** is being asked to dance

VERNA MYERS

sometimes fail. Let's stop aiming for perfection. Let's embrace boldness. Let's assert our ambitions.

INCLUSION SERVING COMPETITIVENESS

As Verna Myers shared, "Diversity is being invited to the party; inclusion is being asked to dance." When aspiring to transform a company into one with impact, surrounding oneself with the right people is one of the first steps. While homogeneous recruitment has led to ingrained habits and stagnation over decades, companies seeking to make a significant impact must recognize that achieving a deeper understanding of society and pursuing sustainable endeavors require a team with diverse talents. Such a team can provide valuable insights into the challenges of our time, particularly as creativity and agility thrive in an environment enriched by diverse talents. This understanding is the foundation for Salesforce's new chapter, as the company aims to build a workplace that reflects the diversity of society. The company organizes an annual summit on representation matters. With their social engagement model 1-1-1 (1% of the company's equity, 1% of services, and 1% of employees' working time dedicated to charitable causes), under Emilie Sidiqian, Salesforce France is going further by enhancing employability through tech apprenticeship programs. The innovative and ambitious "1,000 Women in Tech" initiative aims to empower women to return to work and foster inclusion. The company's mission is to help millions find jobs, with the target of creating 211,300 jobs in France by 2026.

In essence, venturing beyond the usual recruitment pool enables the inclusion of individuals who bring diverse perspectives to present challenges. I must admit that sport brands such as Adidas have the power to change lives with the "no such thing as impossible" attitude. I greatly admire the decision by Adidas several years ago to shift its hiring process by using an online questionnaire instead of traditional CVs.

Focus on inclusivity is also exemplified by Accenture's 34 Accessibility

Centers of Excellence. These centers provide dedicated spaces where individuals with disabilities can test and use a range of assistive technologies and ergonomic equipment, such as headsets, keyboards, and motorized wheelchairs. Beyond keeping the company's own people's interests at heart, this initiative also allows the tech leader (50% of whose executive roles are held by women), to showcase its products to existing and potential clients.[61] Their diversity and inclusion assessment considers factors such as policy perception, commitment, team, and individual feelings.

All these initiatives are examples that purpose-driven companies should urgently adopt. To better understand and engage with society, companies should recruit and welcome diverse profiles.

Dr Anino EMUWA, Founder, 100 Women @Davos

As a trailblazer woman when it comes to inclusive leadership, Anino is an inspiration to me, bringing extraordinary women together at the World Economic Forum to make their voices heard. I love being part of the 100 Women @Davos community, being surrounded by impact-driven women leaders dedicated to creating positive change creates such good vibes!

"It has been increasingly recognized that Diversity, Equity and Inclusion (DE&I) in leadership is associated with improved decision-making and reduced risk-taking, consequently improving the performance of organizations. A McKinsey study showed that the organizations with the most diverse leadership outperformed the least diverse by 25%.

Closing the gender gap also has broader implications on the economy and society. The International Monetary Fund (IMF) refers to gender inequality as macro critical because data shows that closing the gap would contribute to economic growth and stability within the financial sector. The presence of women in leadership is also connected to deeper ESG commitments.

However, despite this compelling research, many organizations are slow to embrace gender-diverse leadership. In light of the increasingly complex challenges facing the world coupled with the rapidly developing technology, which is shaping our lives, all talent must be on board. It is imperative we overcome barriers including supporting the progress of women, create flexible work environment, eliminating wage gaps, and providing paid parental leave.

We need women to have the same opportunities as their male peers to create a sustainable, inclusive and peaceful society where all can thrive."

DIVERSITY, EQUITY, INCLUSION & BELONGING IN ACTION
WHAT IF?

- What is the reality of your company in terms of diversity and inclusion? (by grade and function)?

- What is the gender pay gap for equivalent positions in your company?

- What are your measurable goals regarding Diversity, Equality, and Inclusion? (Gender, Ethnicity, LGBTQIA+, Disability, Generational)

- What actions should be implemented to promote inclusion within your company?

When a brand's **MISSION** aligns with its **ACTIONS**, it becomes a symbol of **HOPE** and **PROGRESS**.

BRANDS
BECOMING SYMBOLS

I n 2017, the platform Jevoteauquotidien.fr was launched. Set up during the French presidential campaign, its founders came up with the idea of having 500 women share their consumption habits, symbolizing the 500 signatories required for each candidate to run for the highest office.[62] The notion that a purchase resembles a vote is a distinct sign that we have moved to a new era. Consumption has increasingly become a civic act through the endorsement of certain brands and rejection of others.

THE RISE OF BOYCOTTS

It must be acknowledged that, over the years, brands have become symbols. They represent an entire value chain that either promotes virtuous growth or strays from it. They play the role of activists, win over distributors, and capture the hearts of consumers. On the other hand, nearly half of the French population has reportedly boycotted a brand before and convinced others to follow suit, to punish actions such as ecosystem degradation, mistreatment, and broader violations of human dignity (racism, discrimination, modern slavery). In France, the primary reasons for consumer boycotts differ somewhat from the rest of Europe, with health concerns being the leading factor, closely followed by animal mistreatment.[63] Major boycott campaigns often stem from scandals like the one that hit Volkswagen when the company was accused of fraudulently manipulating emissions data for its new cars.[64] Most consumers now expect brands to assist them in making more informed choices. Moreover, a majority is willing to pay a premium for products that are more sustainable, responsible, or inclusive.[65] Rihanna's Fenty brands, including both Savage and Fenty Beauty, exemplify inclusivity by challenging conventional norms. Savage features a diverse range of models with bodies of all colors and sizes, while Fenty Beauty offers an extensive makeup shade range to suit every skin tone. Together, these brands represent a powerful commitment to celebrating all forms of beauty, embracing imperfections, and promoting confidence.

AVOIDING GREENWASHING AND ENSURING AUTHENTICITY

As brands increasingly become symbols of societal values, ensuring authenticity in their environmental and social commitments is crucial. Consumer skepticism has risen, making it essential for companies to move beyond superficial gestures and demonstrate genuine dedication.

Greenwashing — where companies exaggerate or fabricate their environmental credentials through misleading public relations and marketing—has become a significant concern. For instance, KLM has faced criticism and even legal action for overselling their sustainability efforts without substantial actions to support those claims.[66] Such practices not only risk damaging a brand's reputation but also undermine the broader movement toward genuine sustainability.

Authenticity requires more than just rhetoric; it demands real, measurable actions aligned with a company's values. Transparent communication about goals, progress, and challenges is vital. True commitment to sustainability involves integrating these principles deeply into a company's operations rather than treating them as an afterthought.

Avoiding greenwashing is about fostering trust and credibility. It involves being honest about where a company stands on its sustainability journey, acknowledging imperfections, and committing to continuous improvement. This approach not only builds stronger relationships with consumers but also contributes meaningfully to a better world.

CHOOSING SOCIALLY ENGAGED BRANDS WITHIN ACTIVIST GROUPS

Society at large is now highly aware of, and responsive to brands' explicit commitments to the issues that matter to them. Therefore, brands have started taking stands against racial injustice for instance, rallying behind slogans like "Black Lives Matter", as seen with Nike, Target, and Netflix. Beyond companies reacting to current events, certain campaigns have left a lasting impact on public opinion and appear to have yielded long-term effects. A case in point is Dove, which launched the *Beauty Without Retouching* campaign which aimed to help girls and women accept themselves, regardless of the look of their skin and its imperfections.

To support this movement, Dove has since provided resources for educators, parents, and young girls, to help each grow their self-esteem and overcome their insecurities. The campaign's impact has been enormous, having reached over 250 million people.[67] Not a day goes by where Dove doesn't receive testimonials from women who have regained their confidence through the resources of the Self-Esteem Project – its training, educational tools for teenagers, and more.

Some brands struck you by the humility that emerges from conscious leaders. Mulberry decided several years ago to incorporate social and environmental aspects into its DNA. Under the leadership of Thierry Andretta, Mulberry committed through initiatives like Made to Last, for a regenerative and circular economy 'from field to wardrobe'. It sets the quality standards at each stage of sourcing and manufacturing of their products, as well as our relationships with the communities around them. This is just the beginning.

CONSUMER-ACTIVISTS AND RETAILERS

Consumers aren't the only ones who are highly sensitive to the impact of brands on the world. Distributors and retailers now also aim to offer their customers products from brands that have proven their positive impact on the world. However, for a brand to convey a message, it must first move beyond a purely transactional relationship with its stakeholders and envision more strategic collaborations, earning their trust and being chosen. This is what Marcelo Behar from Natura & Co did by sharing what the brand is doing to promote diversity-friendly supply chains, rallying local communities in the Amazon especially. With actions come hope.

Building on the discussion of impactful brands, Garnier is a notable example of a company acting as a force for good. Under the leadership of former CEO Adrien Koskas, the brand has not only demonstrated a commitment to positive change but has also achieved its strongest growth in the past twenty years. Garnier has made significant steps forward with its Green Beauty Plan. Not only has the brand decided to publish its own Sustainability Progress Report, but more importantly it has also committed to changing the rules of the game by creating the Environmental Score, which encourages consumers to make more sustainable choices. As it all starts with the products you sell, Garnier has also launched the first Ultra Doux Solid Shampoo. It isn't so easy to encourage new consumer habits. But Garnier's commitment to being a key player of green beauty demonstrates the business case for combining economic performance and environmental excellence.

To conclude, it's essential to mention the brands' symbolic role. Etymologically, the term "symbol" signifies "more than what is seen", referring to an invisible reality which anyone can comprehend. This is precisely what brands should be: signs that the world they want to build is a better version of the current world. Committed brands can then demonstrate their contribution to human progress in every sense of the word – progress towards equality, social justice, environmental preservation, respect for differences, inclusion, and more.

THE COURAGE OF PIONEERING BRANDS

This is how brands become symbols: by representing not only the present but also a vision and plan. It may be more challenging when you are the first mover of an industry.

When I discovered Vestiaire Collective 15 years ago, I instantly became a big fan and advocate. In a world where we are buying more clothes but wearing them less, I admire the work done by co-founder and President Fanny Moizant and CEO Maximilian Bittner. This great team of leaders are here to disrupt consumption behaviors by changing the way people purchase luxury items. I believe the future of fashion is circular. 82% of sold items are a replacement for a first-hand purchase. Buying a used garment extends its life by 2.2 years on average, reducing its carbon, waste, and water footprint by 73%. In a strategy to be net positive, Vestiaire Collective prevents almost three times more emissions than they generate.[68] And, as no company can change the system alone, Vestiaire is now partnering with key brands such as Gucci, Mulberry, Chloe, Alexandre McQueen and more.

Nathalie Roos, CEO, Lipton

The first time we met, Nathalie was at l'Oreal, leading a profound transformation in the hairdressing sector. What struck me was: in a world where ego-driven CEOs are the norm, Nathalie stood out as a genuine leader with a committed approach to empowering people.

"Throughout my career, I have developed a deep conviction that a company can only thrive sustainably if all share its success. This belief has led me to make Creating Value for All my mantra. A leader who embodies this vision guides her or his organization toward economic growth and positively contributes to society and the planet.

At LIPTON Teas and Infusions, I've been leading the transformation of the tea industry. Historically neglected and driven downwards, the market has seen a revival thanks to our commitment to creating value. By offering superior tea experiences, we have not only stimulated demand in both quality and quantity but also managed to redistribute this value throughout the chain—to our customers, business partners, teams, and shareholders. The company has thus become a place of growth for all. Together, we've worked to make Kenya a model of global excellence in tea production by enhancing environmental and social standards.

I anchored all transformations through a strategy centered on Generation Z with its demand for authenticity and immediate action. This generation is serving as a compass for all my decisions. Their voice guides us. For them, action cannot wait. This generation demands a significant and lasting impact, which we can meet by investing in education at the heart of our initiatives and creating authentic alliances. Their inclusion in our strategy is not just a choice but a necessity for our success.

Creating value for everyone is a daily challenge. The key to building long term value is to remain true to our values and defend them at all costs. In a world of constant change, our values are our anchor, reassuring us that we are on the right path. By placing people, education, and innovation at the core of our mission, we build a future where everyone thrives."

MEANINGFUL BRANDS
IN ACTION
WHAT IF?

- How can your brand contribute to a better future?

- In what ways can your brand act as a catalyst for change and become a symbol?

- What do your most conscious consumers expect from you?

- How can you earn the preference of distributors by amplifying their impact?

If we could build
an economy that
would use things
rather than use
them up, we could
BUILD A FUTURE.

ELLEN MAC ARTHUR

THE IMPACT
OF INNOVATION

I n the great revolution we are leading to change our ways of doing things, the epitome of progress is innovation. I believe that the capacity to invent new products or new ways of doing things can solve the major problems plaguing our current model. This is the essence of impact innovation, which not only helps companies succeed in their transformation but also makes them more effective, experiencing growth rates of up to 24%, compared to an average of 4.5% for others.

CIRCULAR ECONOMY VS. LINEAR ECONOMY

Among the profoundly innovative models that are set to revolutionize the business world, the circular economy is perhaps the most symptomatic of the transformations at work. For decades, most consumer-based companies thrived on a linear model. In a nutshell, resources are exploited, products manufactured, and ultimately discarded. This model is clearly extremely detrimental to the planet and results in an enormous amount of waste at the end of the line. The circular economy operates on a different premise, based on the idea that it is possible to preserve natural resources and optimize their use to create reusable, recyclable, or compostable products. It even delves into the realm of regenerative economics, where waste contributes to "natural capital" rather than to the degradation of nature. This is the case with products like Papiefleur's "plantable" cards or materials like PDK (polydiketoenamine), an innovative type of plastic

145

developed at Berkeley in 2019, which can be endlessly reused.

The plastic issue is undeniably one of the most pressing burdens of our time. The trend is evident: if we don't act now, by 2040 plastic production volume will have doubled, and 29 million tons will have been dumped into oceans and waterways.[69] Even more alarming, if we continue at this rate, the weight of plastic waste in the oceans could surpass that of fish by 2050.[70] Reducing plastic packaging must therefore be an absolute priority. British sailor Ellen MacArthur has dedicated her life to this cause. She advocates for at least a 50% reduction of current consumption and for the implementation of a truly circular economy of plastic. This means producing only essential plastic items and making all plastic articles reusable, fully recyclable, or compostable. Achieving this goal requires significant investment in innovation, both in terms of developing new-generation plastics and the necessary recycling infrastructure.

It also appears that the second-hand clothing market will exceed fast fashion soon. For instance, France is the first country in the world "legislating to limit the excesses of Ultra-Fast Fashion".[71] The French National Assembly has taken a monumental step towards tackling the environmental negative impacts of Ultra-Fast Fashion on the Planet. This initiative is a testament to France's commitment to environmental protection and sets a precedent for global action against fast fashion's harmful practices.

This second-hand industry serves as an invitation to major fashion brands to reinvent their model. Farfetch, the world's leading luxury fashion platform, has long positioned itself as a pioneer and innovator. I have learned much from their approach to innovation, previously led by José Neves and his extraordinary teams hoping to reshape the entire luxury sector. Farfetch has introduced three new services: a repair service for damaged items (Farfetch Fix), a second-hand offering (Farfetch Second Life), and a collection service to recycle used items (Farfetch Donate). The challenge lies in reimagining the business model to create a more circular rather than linear approach by 2030.

Who are businesses
really responsible to?
Their customers?
Shareholders? Employees?
We would argue that
it's none of the above.
Fundamentally, businesses
are responsible
to their resource base.
But **WITHOUT A HEALTHY
ENVIRONMENT**, there are
no shareholders,
no employees,
no customers,
and **NO BUSINESS**.

YVON CHOUINARD

Innovation has always been essential for business success. Now, the well-being of the planet and its inhabitants also depends on the transformation of companies. In the fashion industry, there is a need for a massive and intrinsically motivated shift towards a cleaner, more conscious, circular, and inclusive system. The level of change required to address the social and environmental crises we all face is significant. This demands leadership and courage from the entire sector. Brands, retailers, and platforms must set ambitious goals and commit to focusing on and investing in them. All these investments require innovation and leadership. They are designed to meet traditional growth parameters – i.e. revenue growth, customer loyalty through brand affinity – and must also align with investor expectations regarding ESG performance. Other innovative avenues are being explored, from wardrobe rental services to digital productization and virtual try-on technology, to name a few.

TECH AND DATA IN THE SERVICE OF IMPACT

Embedding innovation from the outset to transform the business model remains one of the most common ways to fulfill the company's mission and purpose. Of course, this involves identifying the company's overarching mission, which is closely tied to its core business, and committing to ongoing investments in process improvement and the development of products that positively impact the world In the agri-food sector, for instance, a prime example would be the replacement of pesticides that harm natural ecosystems with pest-resistant seeds — as done by the Nestlé Health Science project. The food giant has embarked on an ambitious program aiming to enhance the health of future generations, leveraging the expertise of over 4,000 R&D experts at the forefront of technological advancements. Their aim is not only to reduce the environmental impact of their production but also to generate genuine positive effects. The company invests €1.7 billion annually in scientific partnerships.[72] Notable advancements include the use of enzymes for recycling Perrier bottles and the development of naturally insect-resistant seeds.

INNOVATION AT THE HEART OF THE BUSINESS MODEL

Sustainable and *social innovation**, in essence, can ultimately serve as the cornerstone of a new business model. Take Decathlon, for example, which has long positioned itself as a pioneer and innovator. Their model focuses on making sports more accessible to all. Creating innovative products is a key component of their value creation, as proven by their use of in-house labs and prototyping workshops exploiting the expertise of the 85 brands under their umbrella. So far, over 3,000 prototypes have been developed, and 95 patents filed.[73] The company's overarching goal remains to offer eco-designed products better tailored to sports perfor-mance at the fairest price. Numerous initiatives have been contributing to this mission, like the Decat'Club, which rewards engaging in sports, purchasing eco-designed products, or participating in environmental actions.

Whether through partnerships or innovative investment, innovation for impact always involves doing things differently to bring about a better world.

Barbara MARTIN COPPOLA, CEO, Decathlon

I have always loved the family-owned business Decathlon and was curious when Barbara joined as the first female CEO of the company from outside of the tribe. We share common values and vision not accepting shortcuts to focus on profitability, convinced that business and purpose must go hand in hand. I fully share Barbara's belief that Change is possible.

"Today, companies have an important role to play in building a prosperous, fair and sustainable world. Our actions should improve lives whilst also preserving the planet. Companies working towards a purpose that benefits a 'greater good' have consistently shown that they can perform better economically, whilst also building a workforce filled with happy and engaged teammates. This has

to be seen and felt by the outside world through meaningful, demonstrable actions. Innovation is fundamental to this. We're breaking new ground, testing new ways of thinking as we pave the way towards our end goal.

Decathlon is striving towards something which goes beyond the traditional economic bottom line, to build a better future for the communities we serve. Colleagues arrive each day filled with the energy and strength that comes from contributing to a greater good. The Decathlon team is made up of 105,000 passionate individuals across 70 different countries. Together, we can be a beacon of light, inspiring other companies to instigate a movement. No mountain is insurmountable.

This is why I joined Decathlon. Our mission is clear: 'To Move People Through the Wonders of Sport.' To do so, we have to protect our collective playground. We place economic and environmental performance on an equal footing, as is reflected by the bonuses given to every employee globally. So, our sales growth is not dependent on worrying CO2 output, we're redesigning every product in a way that'll reduce its impact. At the same time, we've been reimagining Decathlon's core business model by introducing circularity at every stage of the product life cycle. As a result, in 2022, we increased sales by 11% whilst reducing our absolute CO2 output by 1.7%, for the very first time in our history.

Change is possible, we just have to be brave enough to take the first step."

SUSTAINABLE INNOVATION IN ACTION
WHAT IF?

- Is every innovation from your company sustainable by design?

- How far can your business model be reimagined through the lens of a circular economy? How can you bring forward new business models within my company?

- Have you established an ecosystem of startups, experts and partners to guide your innovation efforts?

FINANCE AS A
FORCE FOR GOOD

Blockbusters like *The Wolf of Wall Street* (Martin Scorsese, 2013) ultimately reflect the distorted image which finance holds in the public eye. For too long, finance and sustainable development goals have been disconnected, even pitted against one another. However, as in other areas, times are changing, and financial performance and human progress are no longer at odds. Over the past few years, the financial sector has been shaken up by a much-needed wake-up call. There's an extraordinary momentum at play, as Bertrand Badré, CEO of Blue Like an Orange Sustainable Capital, former Managing Director of the World Bank rightly said, "Finance can save the world". Bertrand has this rare emotional ability to cope with ultracomplex situations and to make these issues accessible for everyone to understand and act upon. We cannot build a sustainable, resilient and inclusive economy without profoundly revisiting the rules that govern its proper functioning: accounting standards, governance, compensation models, fiduciary obligations imposed on managers of our savings, integration of environmental and social dimensions at the core of financial models. He talks about the transition from a 'mark to market' logic to a 'mark to planet' logic." Finance is a copilot to create Better Futures.

DIRECTING INVESTMENT TOWARDS THE COMMON GOOD

In January 2020, BlackRock announced through its CEO a complete shift in its investment strategy towards a focus on responsible investments. Larry Fink stated that, "for companies to thrive over time, they must not only be financially sound, but also show how they positively contribute to society." In doing so, the investment giant is aligning itself with a trend widely shared by most investors, as 88% of them now consider ESG objectives to be as important as financial performance.[74] Moreover, it's noteworthy that the most sustainable companies in terms of their organization and ESG objectives are also the best performers, with a growth rate of 31.5%.[75]

In recent years, investor interest in sustainability has skyrocketed. *Sustainable finance** is becoming a reality. Investors now demand detailed information to understand and track a company's sustainability efforts. Consequently, CFOs and investor relations work hand in hand with CSOs. ESG is gaining ground in deals as investors respond to stakeholder, investor, and future regulatory demand. In fact, KPMG has announced that more than half of investors have canceled M&A deals because of material findings in environmental, social and governance ESG due diligence. Nevertheless, the trend is fragile. The challenge persists. Europe is ahead of the game. As a proof point, Blackrock supported just 4% of the shareholder proposal on environmental and social issues it voted on in 2024, down from 47% in 2021.[76]

REGULATORY EVOLUTION AND RETHINKING PERFORMANCE

Among the levers that have accelerated this shift in perspective, we find the widespread calculation of non-financial performance. European regulations in this regard have made progress. Sustainability and financial reporting go hand in hand. The company's finance department must integrate ESG performance in the reporting process. This is because, logically, the way companies invest will also change due to what is known as the double materiality matrix — evaluating not only the impact of a company's activities on the world but also the impact of the company on its stakeholders. Better data will lead to better decisions, so it is more than reporting, it is about going beyond pledges and shifting words into actions. The cost of inaction is higher than the cost of action. It has a profound economic impact. Last year, the summer heat wave alone across USA, southern Europe and China reduced global GDP by 600 billion dollars.[77]

Therefore, the importance of finance cannot be underestimated; on the contrary, it must be recognized as an extremely powerful conduit for a reconsideration of corporate priorities. In connection with the evolution of standards and the imperative of transparency, companies are therefore strongly encouraged to integrate new dimensions that consider the impact of their decisions on the world and gradually incorporate ESG objectives into investment decisions. Can we invent a new business approach which will account for both human well-being and the health of our planet?

New frameworks are emerging, and I have spent a lot of time searching for the most reliable and tested ones. I must say that the Value Balancing Alliance (VBA) has particularly grabbed my attention. It is a not-for-profit alliance which has developed a methodology to quantify and evaluate the full value created and destroyed by a business model: the economic value, but also the environmental and human and societal value. Thirty multinationals such as Kering, Roche Novartis, SAP, BASF and more are now testing and learning from one another by using this unique methodology. As Chairwoman of their Advisory Board, I am proud to collaborate with pioneering companies to redefine value creation. Much more needs to be done to enable this new narrative, to reshape accounting for better decision-making and encourage leaders to publish their impact statement, i.e. the true value of their company.

It is only a beginning, but a promising one.

"

A company's
long-term
**FINANCIAL
PERFORMANCE**
cannot be
disconnected
from its **SOCIAL
CONSCIENCE.**

"

LARRY FINK

REDEFINING VALUE CREATION

Adopting a more holistic view on corporate value creation is the next step. The concept of 'creating value' has taken on a broader meaning than it once did. Thus, the economic and financial value of an organization is increasingly assessed in terms of its value for society — encompassing ecological performance, reduction of industrial and commercial risks, as well as the ability to engage stakeholders and form consortia. Roles within the finance sector are undergoing significant transformations.

A paradigm shift is needed towards managers less concerned with profit and more with value creation. This vision goes beyond merely integrating non-financial indicators into performance evaluation. The role of finance in the future, much like a change catalyst and transformation facilitator, will be to assist organizations in making the right choices, creating value, better managing performance and impact, and ultimately transcending shareholder-driven logic to create value in every way for its stakeholders. Finance, as a catalyst of change, is now playing a pivotal role in making this change possible. Profit is not the only currency. We must redefine value to include human, social, and environmental aspects.

Therefore, a cultural revolution is underway, driven by a conviction that ESG is not just altruism or philanthropy, but that, on the contrary, these criteria are contrary, factors of immense financial benefits. When the transition to an impact-driven model drives a notable scaling up, there is no longer any reason to delay incorporating impact criteria at the heart of one's model.

Therefore, we are now revising the way we review activities, brands, and countries. The focus used to be on financial performance – revenue and model profitability. Today, the most advanced companies often evaluate their activities based on three criteria: financial performance, operational performance (attributes of the brand, distributor satisfaction, cost-saving plans, employee well-being), and impact performance – contribution to the world and capacity to build a fairer, more sustainable world.

NEW FINANCIAL MECHANISMS

6 out of 9 of our *planetary boundaries** have been reached.[78] Companies are now grappling with a conflict of horizons: short-term priorities demand immediate decisions within a well-defined framework, while long-term goals require investing human and financial resources toward uncertain outcomes. Two steps are critical to enable a shift from the former to the latter. The first one is protecting financial resources to support the execution of the social and environmental agenda. The second step is connecting solutions to the brands and products to enable a competitive edge.

New financial tools are now available for companies to direct their investments towards sustainable models. Of course, many companies have already integrated carbon impact into their investment strategy. Their number has grown steadily since 2017, now surpassing seventy. Many companies have also started to implement an internal price for carbon. It is often a synthetic value, mostly used during the approval process for investments. The impact of increasing or decreasing emissions is monetized and included in future cashflows estimates. For example, BEL's investment committee regularly reviews the company's internal carbon price. BEL is also using the metric to calculate its quarterly Results on Operations for its main businesses.

In recent years, the issuance of so-called Green Bonds, also commonly known as sustainability bonds, have helped compel companies to reduce their carbon footprint or improve packaging recyclability. It is also worth mentioning loans from the Public Investment Bank, which now provide new facilities for SMEs that have incorporated the impact of their activities on the environment and society into their models.

Another new model is emerging — that of Corporate Impact Funds. For example, Microsoft has created a Climate Innovation Fund that exclusively invests in activities which have a positive impact on climate or actively combat climate change. Danone, through its Livelihoods and Ecosystem

Funds, has been developing a similar approach quite a long time now.

Often, these funds operate independently of brands and business operations. To develop impact-driven companies, the challenge lies in intricately connecting these funds with the brands themselves. Unilever has successfully done this with the creation of the Unilever Nature and Climate Fund, set up by Éric Soubeiran, a passionate mountain enthusiast and exceptional leader whom I greatly enjoy collaborating with. The initiative encompasses €1 billion funded by the group's brands with the objective to invest in projects that have both a high potential for value creation and tangible benefits for the planet.[79] Since this fund is financed by brand profits, it places sustainable development and consumer messaging at the heart of Unilever's dynamics, thereby clearly directing the group's investments. The fund's programs, in partnership with the Knorr brand, now ensures that 80% of the ingredients in Knorr's soups and other products are sourced from regenerative agriculture.[80] To go further, Unilever has even partnered with AXA and Tikehau Capital to jointly create a fund dedicated to regenerative agriculture. The goal is to accelerate the speed and scale of these projects by putting together their respective resources, expertise, and strengths, to address the long-term financing needs for these transformations to happen.

A future challenge will not only be to protect nature but also to learn to value it properly. This is the path taken by the Intrinsic Exchange Group, which commits to creating value without exploiting nature, but rather by considering it as an asset.

The question is: how fast can we make the change happen?

Christophe BABULE, Chief Financial Officer, L'Oréal Group

Passionate about sailing, Christophe set the course to redefine performance. He is a pioneer, a visionary leader when it comes to finance as a force for good. Christophe brings kindness to everyone, an authentic leader, a spark to bring people along.

"In today's world, finance must be more than a tool for profit — it needs to be a force for good. I believe finance plays a pivotal role when it comes to business contribution for positive change. Over the past 30 years, starting from my first role in Italy, I've seen how leadership in finance can fuel purpose-driven growth. From my experiences across China, Mexico, and Paris, I've gained a profound appreciation for creating value for all, for our shareholders but also our stakeholders, which now shape my vision for finance at L'Oréal.

As the world is moving from a shareholder primacy to stakeholder capitalism, businesses need to do good while doing well. Value creation is becoming the new currency. More than ever, finance can act as a catalyst for value creation — supporting business to thrive in ways that uplift both people and the planet. I believe it is our responsibility to ensure that finance contributes to creating value that benefits not only our business but also our communities and the environment. This is why I see my role evolving from Chief Financial Officer to Chief Value Creation Officer, where my mission is to embed purpose into every decision we make, creating value for all. To my fellow leaders, this requires courage and determination. The world is demanding more from us, and only businesses that put purpose at the core of their strategies will succeed. Finance is no longer just about economic performance; it's about creating a future we can all be proud of."

FINANCE FOR GOOD
IN ACTION
WHAT IF?

- What if you were to shift from P&L (Profit and Loss) management to value creation management?

- What criteria can you use to evaluate non-financial performance?

- What financial mechanisms can you use to enable the scaling of positive impact initiatives? How do these connect with the company's associated brand(s)?

Individually, we are one **DROP**. Together, we are an **OCEAN**.

RYUNOSUKE SATORO

SAVING THE WORLD:
A COLLECTIVE ENDEAVOR

I close this essay on a subject that deeply resonates with me – that of business coalitions working together to achieve more. I'm reminded of J.R.R Tolkien's epic saga, *The Lord of the Rings*. If we take each group of characters individually — the Hobbits, the Elves, the Dwarves, the Men, and the Wizards — we understand that none of them could have overcome the power of Sauron on their own. However, for all their differences and varied backgrounds, their unlikely alliance was what ultimately overthrew this malevolent power. To me, the strength of the Fellowship of the Ring resembles that of business coalitions. Regardless of their size, industry, or background, companies amplify their positive impact on the world when they come together to imagine new ways of doing things.

COALITIONS AS THE NEW NORM

Our world is facing enormous challenges: global warming, biodiversity erosion, and legitimate demands for social justice. Thinking that anyone can reverse such trends on their own is an illusion. These structural, cultural, and operational challenges call for a collective mobilization, primarily from companies. That's why the financial world must now think about economic coalitions: shifting from a competitive mindset to a cooperative one. To magnify the impact of a decision and make it truly effective, it's necessary to collaborate with other actors in the industry where one operates. This requires transcending our usual competitive logic to achieve a common

objective. Strategic alliances can drive innovation, address common challenges, and create value for all.

For instance, under the stewardship of Nicolas Hieronimus (a CEO deeply
committed to leadership) L'Oréal teamed up last September with Henkel,
LVMH, Natura & Co, and Unilever to launch the Eco-Score system. This
system evaluates the environmental impact of hygiene and beauty products,
similarly to how the Nutri-Score system informs consumers about the
health impact of food products. This scientific approach, open to all companies in the sector, addresses consumer demands for transparency. It is
an example of how collaboration can yield results across all fields. From
influencing public policies — such as banning junk food in schools — to
climate commitments, unity is a force. Furthermore, an action coalition
among companies in the same sector not only avoids creating competitive distortions but also effectively shifts the entirety of a system towards
impact. Among numerous examples, the Fashion Pact is a notable international coalition aiming to redefine the fashion sector. By signing this
pact, 60 CEO's, representing 160 companies committed to goals like
eliminating plastic use in B2C by 2025 and in B2B by 2030.[81]

The time has passed when one could do it alone. Today, the focus has
shifted from merely enhancing a brand's image to adopting a long-term
perspective that drives tangible change. Given the immense mission and
critical stakes, competitors have begun to join forces, companies are
engaging in dialogue with governments, and consumer coalitions are making
radical choices (i.e. the previously discussed boycott and support decisions). To pool knowledge, resources, and expertise, companies such as
Sanofi, Orange, Capgemini, and Generali have come together as a united
front. With a European e-health incubator named Future4Care, endowed
with a budget of €24 million, they aim to further digital health services,
support medical deserts, and provide healthcare globally.[82]

FROM THINK TANKS TO ACT TANKS

It is also important to recognize that government support is crucial to facilitate change and reward virtuous practices, while lifting the least performant companies upwards — much like how the quota system helped accelerate gender diversity in several professions. What companies now await are clear and transparent signals through robust regulation and widespread fiscal incentives, which would further encourage them to shift their perspectives. I personally believe that instead of a punitive system, we should envision tangible ways to reward top performers through the lever of taxation.

Yes, collaborative action — involving governments, major institutions, and NGOs — is indispensable for resolving the pressing challenges of our time. However, I now believe that the reimagination of our models rests in the hands of businesses. They possess the power to act. We stand at a crossroads: the cost of inaction will soon surpass that of action. Therefore, companies no longer have a choice; they must create meaning, place sustainability at the core of their business models, and demonstrate their contibution to a better world.

Growing populations worldwide are straining healthcare systems: people are living longer, chronic diseases are on the rise, and infectious diseases remain a threat. Health is a basic human right. This is the reason why Roche, under the leadership of Rolf Hoenger, set up a cross-industry collaboration with Microsoft, Siemens Healthineers, Copenhagen Institute for Future Studies. The Movement Health Foundation thrives on fostering inclusive partnerships that unite private and public entities, an ACT TANK is about real life on the ground experience to learn and innovate. It is about bringing digital solutions to scale on cancer and cardiovascular diseases. Every person should have the opportunity to benefit from great leaps forward in science and technology and not have their life and health defined by their circumstances.

THE COURAGE TO SPEAK, THE COURAGE TO ACT

So, with so many good potential initiatives at hand, why does it remain challenging to shift the trajectory on a large scale? Scientists are clear: our planet is overheating, resources are depleting, biodiversity is declining, polar ice is melting, and social injustices are intensifying. If businesses have the power to implement change more swiftly than governments, what has been hindering their progress? Why is there such a gap between words and actions, commitments and reality?

Given the urgency of these questions and the question mark outcome of COPs, I co-founded Generation Glasgow with entrepreneurs Dimitri Caudrelier, former CEO of Quantis and Emmanuelle Duez as the founder of The Boson Project. This collective of leaders brings together individuals from over 30 organizations — including companies, NGOs, and academics — to tangibly address the obstacles still hindering transition. We've chosen to decipher both the remaining reluctances as well as the virtues necessary for ushering in a new era, in a context where the current approaches still fall short. Together, we've analyzed the main stumbling blocks and concluded that a cultural revolution is necessary to make corporate culture evolve by utilizing its members' goodwill. At the forefront of this cultural revolution comes the topic of governance changes. A long way to go but with collective actions come hope.

IT ALL COMES DOWN TO LEADERSHIP

You don't need to do it alone. It may sometimes feel scary, but the only way to move towards a successful future is to reimagine the economic system. I believe there will be no transformation without a leadership committed to broad changes. There is no strategy without convictions. But a conviction without action remains a dream, an idea. A leader's conviction without collective action remains small, unable to reach the necessary speed and scale.

As a guest speaker at the 2023 Davos World Economic Forum and member of the 100 Women @ Davos, I remember Al Gore's words on our responsibility as leaders clearly. Young people around the world are looking at those in positions of power. They struggle with the inconsistency of decision-makers. We need to stop twiddling our thumbs and change the rules of the game. We need to reform world institutions. We need to take charge of our destiny and rebuild trust with the young generation. We need to give people hope. I believe political rhetoric will not succeed on its own. We need this new generation of (business) leaders to act every day for a better future. We need new leaders who are eager to drive change and put positive impact at the heart of their business models. The question is not "why?" anymore but "how?" Nothing will happen without leadership. It is a human journey. So, what type of leader do you want to be? What do you stand for? And how will you build trust to pave the way for a better future?

Sandrine Dixson-Declève, Co-President, The Club of Rome

When you think about a Change Maker, who is acting everyday fearlessly to push the boundaries for sustainable futures, you think about Sandrine. I have the pleasure of meeting Sandrine several times per year to encourage systems shift. Whenever I am with her, I feel so energized, she cultivates my inner light. We need more heart in leadership. She is an inspiration for all of us around the world to become better versions of ourselves.

"We must collectively address the fact that we are faced with the greatest existential challenges of the 21st century. This entails both enhancing partnerships as well as bringing more people on the journey of change. Creating new narratives and anchoring the change ethos into both evidence-based decision making, personal sense making and place-based action.

The complex challenges before us today necessitate new bold cooperation and partnership models that understand the speed and scale of action required towards alternative futures. Alternative futures like the Giant Leap scenario in Earth4All that shows us that creating an operating space within the planetary boundaries is only possible if we dramatically reduce poverty and inequality and that we enhance collective trust to work together towards a common goal.

This means breaking down silos and engaging in difficult conversations and joint action systemically across continents, countries, cities, government departments, political parties, sectors, generations, and disciplines. It will necessitate unpacking deep blind spots and getting to the root cause of our crises from shifting our current neo liberal extractive and over financialized economic model and neo colonial global financial architecture to regenerative models that place a value on human, natural and financial capital at the same time. Most importantly, it will mean hard wiring humanity into all we do with a deep respect and acknowledgement of the broader planetary ecosystem and a new sense of purpose that shifts the conversation from the "me" to the "we" and from the "ego" to the "eco". I fundamentally believe that human beings can both be wise and good, but without such shifts in mindset and readiness to embrace profound systems change we will not reach our planetary or humanitarian goals."

PARTNERSHIP & COALITION IN ACTION
WHAT IF?

- What groups of like-minded leaders—within your industry, geographical region, or areas of interest—could you join to gain strength and optimism, share best practices, and collaborate on common goals?

- What are the challenges within your business that would require alliances to shift the system?

- What could motivate your peers to come together to drive change in your sector or industry?

GOODNESS is the quality of being **KIND**, **HELPFUL**, and **HONEST**. It can refer to an organization's or a person's actions and behaviors. It is about being **GENEROUS TO BUILD A WORLD FOR PEOPLE AND PLANET TO THRIVE**. It retains faith in human goodness.

CONCLUSION

The world needs new common standards to make change happen. These are critical to benchmark and incentivize virtuous models. But metrics alone are not sufficient to make that shift happen.

More than ever, the world needs courageous leaders. We are at a crossroads. To develop more virtuous models, companies need to reinvent themselves and demonstrate what they contribute to society. But it's not that easy. Every time I meet leaders, business executives, pioneers of the economic transition, or industry frontrunners, I realize how challenging transformation is. The amount of energy, conviction, and determination required to lead an entire organization along this demanding path is substantial.

Enlightened, visionary, and courageous leaders do exist. They are out there, pioneering virtuous models, being trailblazers, making positive impact the compass of their decision-making. They commit with head and heart, giving back, being grateful, honest, and humble throughout the journey, as true transformation requires a shift in cultural paradigm. These leaders never shy away from the challenges of a system change. They harness the power of people and partners to implement genuine transformations. Cooperation is becoming the new norm. Courage is more than just a virtue. It is a necessity when it comes to the fortitude required to face challenging times.

To lead this transformation, one should not strive for perfection — far from it — but rather decide to align their words and actions, their beliefs and decisions, their ambitions and resources. This requires embracing the need to learn at every stage and striving for alignment of all crucial parameters. This requires the courage to place not only one's business but also oneself in the service of the common good, not only today but also in the future.

It is for these courageous leaders that I founded Goodness & Co., to support those who will make a difference tomorrow, to encourage those who are ready to reshape the landscape of their industry. This journey from the mind to the heart is made possible by all the women and men who are willing to take the leap. In Gandhi's words, "Be the change that you wish to see in the world."

This, for me, is the audacity we need.

In a few years from now, I want to be among those who can look into their children's eyes and say that they did their best at a moment when it truly mattered.

GLOSSARY

B Corporation

The B Corp movement brings together companies that aim not to be the best in the world, but the best for the world. B Corp companies seek to shift the economy from a shareholder-driven system to a stakeholder-driven one, creating value for all the company's stakeholders of the company. The B Corp movement already counts 9,000 certified companies across 102 countries, including over 400 in France and 2000 in the UK. Additionally, it inspires over 280,000 companies that use the B Impact Assessment to evaluate, manage, and further their positive impact on the world.[83]

Biodiversity

Biodiversity refers to the wealth represented by all living beings, from plants to animals. Preserving biodiversity is a major global challenge, just as important as combating pollution or climate change – especially because natural habitats are the first to be threatened by these phenomena, as well as by human activities. Bees, for example, are often cited as an endangered species, a problem all the more pressing that they play an essential role in preserving ecosystem balance through pollination.

Circular Economy

The circular economy is a more sustainable and regenerative economic model based on the respect of our planet's boundaries. It creates a virtuous cycle based on minimal resource consumption, recycling, and waste reduction during production cycles. A prime example of a circular economy practice is the reuse of recycled plastic for other purposes within the value chain.

Climate Emergency

This expression encompasses a common understanding that we must quickly slow down the global warming caused by human activities. Experts and policymakers agree that this rise in temperature should be kept below 2°C by the end of the century to prevent a climate collapse which would also have tremendous social and economic consequences. However, according to the latest IPCC report, without new climate policies, global warming could reach 2.2 to 3.5°C. To keep it under the critical threshold, CO2 emissions must be reduced by at least 43% by 2030.[84]

Coalition

Given the gravity of the challenges we are facing, no single company can succeed alone. In this context, there has been a growing trend in recent years towards partnerships and alliances that bring organizations together around a common goal. These coalitions can emerge within the same sector, even among competitors, in order to enable the transition towards new models for real change. Alone, you might go faster; together, you can go further.

Corporate Social Responsibility (CSR)

Corporate Social Responsibility refers to a company's consideration of environmental and social issues within its activities. It includes ethical business practices and stakeholders' engagement.

Courage

Courage is an essential value for any leader embarking on the positive transformation of their company. The courage to think big, the courage to act, the courage to let go – all these are manifestations of this cardinal value. What these forms of courage have in common is the strength of heart, the fortitude that manifests in challenging situations that require tough decisions, sometimes painful choices.

Diversity, Equity, Inclusion and Belonging (DEIB)

Diversity, Equity, Inclusion and Belonging refer to an ensemble of policies, strategies, and practices that aim to create and maintain a professional environment which promotes the hiring of socially diverse profiles, fair treatment for all, and the empowerment of everyone involved in the life of an organization. Ultimately, it's about promoting equal opportunities regardless of an individual's gender, disability, sexual orientation, cultural background, or age. Every step count, from recruitment to talent development. But there is still a long way to go to achieve gender parity in governance bodies or truly inclusive management.

Empowerment

To empower is to inspire, ignite, drive, animate, encourage and engage. To transition from intention to action, the rallying of all is key, and turning everyone into agents of change is essential to drive the cultural revolution the world is in dire need of.

Environmental, Social and Governance (ESG)

ESG encompasses the three criteria used to assess a company's impact on the environment and society within the context of its non-financial analysis. Once a marginal phenomenon, the consideration of such criteria is now strongly encouraged by legislators. Since January 2022, incorporating sustainability indicators in reporting has become mandatory for companies with more than 500 employees in the EU.

Goodness

Goodness is the quality of being kind, helpful, and honest. It can refer to an organization's or a person's actions and behaviors. It is about having the generosity to work towards building a world where both humans and the planet to thrive, where we can retain a faith in human goodness.

Governance

Governance commonly refers to the people, rules, and laws that direct and control a company for the long term while protecting the interests of stakeholders. In a purpose-driven company, governance is also the driving force behind the shift from a shareholder-oriented logic to a stakeholder-oriented one. The challenge lies in establishing an inclusive and collaborative governance model that can be the true driver of transformation.

Greenwashing

Greenwashing occurs when companies exaggerate or fabricate their environmental credentials deceptively using green public relations and marketing tactics to convince the public that its products, goals, or policies are environmentally friendly.

Mission-Driven Company

The mission-driven company is a legal framework introduced in France in 2019 through the PACTE Law. It refers to a company which stands for something bigger than its products and services. The mission-driven company integrates its purpose and environmental commitments in its bylaws. The philosophy behind mission-driven companies can be summarized as the belief in the compatibility of a pursuit of the common good and economic performance. As of now, France has nearly 1200 mission-driven companies, and this is just the beginning.

Planetary Boundaries

These are the phenomena which must be monitored and limited to ensure the survival of life on Earth. There are nine of them: climate change, biodiversity loss, disruption of nitrogen and phosphorus cycles, soil depletion, introduction of new substances, freshwater use, ocean acidification, ozone layer degradation, and atmospheric aerosol increase. Today, six of these boundaries have been exceeded.

Purpose

The company's purpose is the company's raison d'être, the reason for its existence beyond mere profit generation. In significant strategic decisions and daily operations, the company's purpose is like a guiding star that informs choices and rallies stakeholders around a shared destiny. Choosing a purpose is crucial because it must come from the heart of employees and those surrounding the company to be effective, resonating with the company's activities, determining its uniqueness, and revealing its core culture and values. In France, since the 2019 PACTE Law, companies can now include their purpose in their bylaws.

Purpose-led Company

The challenge taken up by a purpose-led company is to create a virtuous model that generates a net positive impact. A purpose-le company decides to give more than it takes. It essentially involves rethinking one's business model by considering its consequences on society and the planet. In other words, the time has come to invent a company that positively contributes to progress, consistently creating not only wealth for shareholders but also value for all stakeholders.

Regenerative Economy

A regenerative economy develops virtuous models which visibly contribute to the common good. Its key principles can be summarized as the most efficient use of resources possible and a focus on local economy to promote proximity exchanges fostering cooperation rather than competition. In a way, a company that embraces a regenerative model produces more value than it consumes.

Sustainable Finance

Sustainable finance is a structural means of addressing current challenges by reconciling economic performance and positive impact on the world. To support long-term projects, sustainable finance prioritizes financial operations that consider the extra-financial criteria of ESG.

Social Innovation

Social innovation develops new responses to social needs that the market or governments alone cannot address. It's a lever for change that balances economic performance and contribution to the common good, primarily in strategic sectors like early childhood, health, poverty alleviation, exclusion, or discrimination.

Social Justice

Social justice is the socio-political goal of achieving equal rights for all peoples and the possibility for all humans to benefit, without discrimination, from economic and social progress worldwide. Therefore, there can be no true economic progress without social justice.

Vision

The company's vision corresponds to its philosophy and, more concretely, the direction in which it projects itself into the future. It's like the summit of a mountain one is aiming to climb. Unlike an objective, it's not a goal to achieve but rather a framework for thought and action, a trajectory geared to the future.

NOTES

1. Italicized words and phrases that are followed by an asterisk are defined in the glossary.

2. Ministry of Culture. (n.d.). *The general tax system.* https://www.culture.gouv.fr/en/Thematic/patronage/Companies/The-general-tax-system

3. *Wealth of five richest men doubles since 2020, as wealth of five billion people falls.* (2024, January 15). Oxfam GB. https://www.oxfam.org.uk/media/press-releases/wealth-of-five-richest-men-doubles-since-2020-as-wealth-of-five-billion-people-falls/#:~:text=The%20world's%20five%20richest%20men,global%20corporate%20power%20has%20found.

4. *Plastic in the Ocean Statistics.* (n.d). Condor Ferries. https://www.condorferries.co.uk/plastic-in-the-ocean-statistics

5. *WWF Living Planet Report : Devastating 69 % drop in wildlife populations.* (2022, October 13). WWF. https://www.wwf.eu/?7780966/WWF-Living-Planet-Report-Devastating-69-drop-in-wildlife-populations-since-1970#:~:text=Wildlife%20populations%20%2D%20mammals%2C%20birds%2C,Planet%20Report%20(LPR)%202022.

6. *KPMG 2023 CEO Outlook.* (2023, September 6). KPMG. https://kpmg.com/xx/en/home/insights/2023/09/kpmg-global-ceo-outlook-survey.html

7. Edelman. (2023, January 15). *2023 Edelman Trust Barometer. Global Report.* https://www.edelman.com/sites/g/files/aatuss191/files/2023-03/2023%20Edelman%20Trust%20Barometer%20Global%20Report%20FINAL.pdf

8. Cave, D. (2022, July 14). *Majority of candidates would reject job offer if employer didn't support diversity, research finds.* People Management. https://www.peoplemanagement.co.uk/article/1793094/majority-candidates-reject-job-offer-employer-didnt-support-diversity-research-finds

9. Confino, J. (2014, September 23). *Sustainability corporations perform better financially, report finds.* The Guardian. https://www.theguardian.com/sustainable-business/2014/sep/23/business-companies-profit-cdp-report-climate-change-sustainability

10. Singal, N. (2021, November 14). *Unilever saved 1.2 billion of cost due to sustainable sourcing, eco-efficiencies at factories.* Business Today. https://www.businesstoday.in/latest/corporate/story/unilever-saved-eu12-billion-of-cost-due-to-sustainable-sourcing-eco-efficiencies-at-factories-312105-2021-11-13

11. Foucart, S. (2023, February 11). *European insect populations tumble.* Le Monde. https://www.lemonde.fr/en/international/article/2023/02/11/european-insect-populations-tumble_6015288_4.html#:~:text=Recent%20studies%20point%20out%20declines,human%20activities%20and%20intensive%20agriculture.

12. Jones, B. (2024, May 16). *The end of coral reefs as we know them.* Vox. https://www.vox.com/climate/24137250/coral-reefs-bleaching-climate-change#

13. *The second-hand luxury market : key figures, trends and challenges in 2024.* (2024, January 25). Tripartie. https://tripartie.com/en/toolkit/second-hand-luxury-market-figures/#:~:text=The%20second%2Dhand%20luxury%20market%20has%20expanded%20markedly%2C%20from%20%E2%82%AC,in%20the%20last%2012%20months.

14. *Kering commits to next horizon in sustainability with group-wide target for reducing absolute emissions by 40%*. (2023, March 17). Kering. https://www.kering.com/en/news/kering-commits-to-next-horizon-in-sustainability-with-group-wide-target-for-reducing-absolute-emissions-by-40/

15. Polman, P., Winston, A. (2024, August 21). *Stakeholder Capitalism Still Makes Business Sense*. Harvard Business Review. https://hbr.org/2024/08/stakeholder-capitalism-still-makes-business-sense

16. Robinson-Tillett, S. (2024, March 11). *SBTi axes net zero commitments of 200+ companies - Real Economy Progress*. Real Economy Progress. https://real-economy-progress.com/climate/sbti-axes-net-zero-commitments-of-200-companies/

17. Heraud, B. (2020, April 8). *Face à la crise du Covid-19, les stratégies des entreprises les plus responsables et durables sont payantes*. Novethic. https://www.novethic.fr/actualite/entreprises-responsables/entreprise-responsable/isr-rse/face-a-la-crise-du-covid-19-les-strategies-durables-des-entreprises-sont-payantes-148420.html

18. Mollet, C. (2024, March 26). *Septième portrait des sociétés à mission*. Observatoire des Sociétés À Mission. https://www.observatoiredessocietesamission.com/barometres-osam/septieme-portrait-des-societes-a-mission/

19. Moressa, S. (2021, February 25). *Camif se félicite d'une croissance de 44 % en 2020*. Univers Habitat. https://www.univers-habitat.eu/blanc-brun/2021/02/25/camif-se-felicite-d-une-croissance-de-44-en-2020_9047/

20. Doctolib. (2024). *Impact Report France*. https://media.doctolib.com/image/upload/mkg/file/impact_report_en_digital.pdf

21. *En 2023, Doctolib devient "entreprise à mission" et investit 92 millions d'euros dans l'innovation*. (2023, January 30). Doctolib. https://about.doctolib.fr/news/en-2023-doctolib-devient-entreprise-a-mission-et-investit-92-millions-deuros-dans-linnovation/

22. *B Lab Global Site*. (n.d). https://www.bcorporation.net/en-us/

23. Schwimmer, S. (2023, December 15). *Reflecting on our impact in 2023*. B Corp. https://www.bcorporation.net/en-us/news/blog/reflecting-on-our-impact-in-2023/

24. O'Leary, J., Whittaker, M. (2022, August 11). *Why trust is key to leading companies unlocking value*. World Economic Forum. https://www.weforum.org/agenda/2022/08/why-trust-is-key-to-leading-companies-unlocking-value/

25. Edelman Trust Management. (n.d.). Retrieved from https://www.edelman.com/trust/edelman-trust-management

26. *Act for Food: Au-delà des discoursm Carrefour veut « crédibiliser sa démarche durable »*.(2019, July 4). Novethic. https://www.novethic.fr/actualite/social/consommation/isr-rse/act-for-good-au-dela-des-discours-carrefour-veut-credibiliser-sa-demarche-durable-147443.html

27. *Carrefour teams up with seven industrial partners to launch an international coalition to boost sales of alternative plant-based products*. (2023, September 6). Carrefour Group. https://www.carrefour.com/en/news/2023/carrefour-lance-une-coalition-internationale-pour-accelerer-les-ventes-dalternatives

28. Dhingra, N., Samo, A., Schaninger, B., & Schrimper, M. (2021, April 5). *Help your employees find purpose—or watch them leave*. McKinsey & Company. https://www.mckinsey.com/capabilities/people-and-organizational-performance/our-insights/help-your-employees-find-purpose-or-watch-them-leave

29. Deloitte. (2024). *2024 Gen Z and Millennial Survey: Living and working with purpose in a*

transformative world. https://www2.deloitte.com/content/dam/Deloitte/at/Documents/presse/at-deloitte-global-gen-z-millennial-survey-gesamte-studie.pdf

30. Khourym G., Crabtree, S. (2019, February 6), *Are Businesses Worldwide Suffering From a Trust Crisis?* Gallup. *https://www.gallup.com/workplace/246194/businesses-worldwide-suffering-trust-crisis.aspx*

31. Duncan, P., & Butler, P. (2023, November 24). *Depression in British adults doubles during coronavirus crisis.* The Guardian. https://www.theguardian.com/society/2020/aug/18/depression-in-british-adults-doubles-during-coronavirus-crisis

32. ESG News. (2024, May 16). *Nearly half of Gen Z and millennials reject employers over climate concerns: Deloitte survey.* https://esgnews.com/nearly-half-of-gen-z-and-millennials-reject-employers-over-climate-concerns-deloitte-survey/

33. Jordan, J., Sorell, M. (2019, June 4*). Why You Should Create a "Shadow Board" of Younger Employees.* Harvard Business Review. https://hbr.org/2019/06/why-you-should-create-a-shadow-board-of-younger-employees

34. Boffa-Comby, P. (2021, April 01). *Il suffit de 10% des collaborateurs pour changer toute l'entreprise.* Harvard Business Review. https://www.hbrfrance.fr/chroniques-experts/2019/09/27890-il-suffit-de-10-des-collaborateurs-pour-changer-toute-lentreprise/

35. *Strategies for effective sustainability in corporate governance.* (2024, July 16). FinTech Global. https://fintech.global/2024/07/16/strategies-for-effective-sustainability-in-corporate-governance/#:~:text=The%20Competence%20Barrier%20While%2091,sustainability%20at%20the%20board%20level.

36. Soonieus, R., Woods, W., Young, D., Tatar, S. (2022, March), *Directors Can Up Their Game on Environmental. Social, and Governance Issues.* The BCG-INSEAD Board ESG Pulse Check. https://www.insead.edu/system/files?file=2023-05/directors-can-up-their-game-on-environmental-social-and-governance-issues-march2022.pdf&

37. Batish, A. (2024, June 24). *Q1 2024 Equilar Gender Diversity Index.* Equilar. https://www.equilar.com/reports/112-q1-2024-equilar-gender-diversity-index.html

38. Tonello, M. (2023, December 7). *The Recent Trends in Board Compositions and Refreshment in the Russell 3000 and S&P 500.* Harvard Law School Forum on Corporate Governance. https://corpgov.law.harvard.edu/2023/12/07/recent-trends-in-board-composition-and-refreshment-in-the-russell-3000-and-sp-500/#:~:text=In%20the%20S%26P%20500%2C%20it,years%20in%20the%20Russell%203000).

39. KPMG. (2022). *Poised for Change? Boardroom Diversity Survey 2021.* https://assets.kpmg.com/content/dam/kpmg/sg/pdf/2022/05/kpmg-bgi-boardroom-diversity-survey-2021.pdf

40. *New Kroll Study Shows Stronger Investment Returns for Companies with High ESG Ratings.* (2023, September 13). Kroll. https://www.kroll.com/en/about-us/news/kroll-study-shows-stronger-investment-returns-companies-high-esg-ratings

41. *Faire de la RSE une ambition et un atout pour chaque entreprise - Sénat.* (2022, 27 octobre). Sénat. https://www.senat.fr/rap/r22-089/r22-08911.html

42. High, P. (2020, May 26*). Who Led Your Digital Transformation? Your CIO Or COVID-19?* Forbes. https://www.forbes.com/sites/peterhigh/2020/05/26/who-led-your-digital-transformation-your-cio-or-covid-19/

43. *New CDP data shows companies are recognizing the need for climate transition plans but are*

not moving fast enough amidst incoming mandatory disclosure. (2023, February 16). CDP. https://www.cdp.net/en/articles/climate/new-cdp-data-shows-companies-are-recognizing-the-need-for-climate-transition-plans-but-are-not-moving-fast-enough-amidst-incoming-mandatory-disclosure

44. Mace, M. (2023, February 27). *More than 75% of major companies linking carbon targets to executive pay.* Edie. https://www.edie.net/more-than-75-of-major-companies-linking-carbon-targets-to-executive-pay/

45. Saint-Exupéry, A. de. (1942). *Flight to Arras. translated by Lewis Galantière.* Harcourt, Brace & World.

46. World Economic Forum. (2023, June 20). *Global gender gap report 2023.* https://www.weforum.org/publications/global-gender-gap-report-2023/

47. OECD. (2023). *Gender equality and work.* https://www.oecd.org/en/topics/sub-issues/gender-equality-and-work.html

48. World Economic Forum. (2023, June 20) *Gender equality is stalling: 131 years to close the gap.* https://www.weforum.org/press/2023/06/gender-equality-is-stalling-131-years-to-close-the-gap/

49. World Economic Forum. (2023, June 20). Global Gender Gap Report 2023. https://www3.weforum.org/docs/WEF_GGGR_2023.pdf

50. Taaffe-Maguire, S. (2022, October 4). *Glacially slow progress on gender equality as 96% of CEOS of Britain's largest public companies are men.* Sky News. https://news.sky.com/story/glacially-slow-progress-on-gender-equality-as-96-of-ceos-of-britains-largest-public-companies-are-men-12711481

51. Elting, L. (2023, January 27). *New Year, New Glass Heights: Women now comprise 10% of top U.S. corporation CEOs.* Forbes. https://www.forbes.com/sites/lizelting/2023/01/27/new-year-new-glass-heights-for-the-first-time-in-history-over-10-of-fortune-500-ceos-are-women/

52. France 24. (2024, March 5). *Women battle on for equality in top business jobs.* https://www.france24.com/en/live-news/20240305-women-battle-on-for-equality-in-top-business-jobs

53. Mirova Foundation. (2022, April 22). *What if we asked men and women... the same questions? - SISTA x Mirova Forward.* YouTube. https://www.youtube.com/watch?v=fMwHV3JGrNI

54. Ministère Chargé de l'Égalité entre les Femmes et les Hommes et de la Lutte Contre les Discriminations. (2021, October 25). *Résultats de la 8ème édition du Palmarès de la Féminisation des instances dirigeantes des entreprises du SBF120 - 25.10.2021: égalité-femmes-hommes.* https://www.egalite-femmes-hommes.gouv.fr/cp-resultats-de-la-8eme-edition-du-palmares-de-la-feminisation-des-instances-dirigeantes-des-entreprises-du-sbf120-25-10-2021#:~:text=Le%20classement%202020%20confirme%20une,5%20points%20en%20un%20an).

55. Huet, N. (2022, June 8). *EU strikes deal to impose 40% quota for women on boards of large companies by 2026.* Euronews. https://www.euronews.com/next/2022/06/08/eu-strikes-deal-to-impose-40-per-cent-quota-for-women-on-boards-of-large-companies-by-2026

56. Dixon-Fyle, S., Dolan, K., Hunt, D. V., & Prince, S. (2020, May 19). *Diversity wins: How inclusion matters.* McKinsey & Company. https://www.mckinsey.com/featured-insights/diversity-and-inclusion/diversity-wins-how-inclusion-matters

57. Scikey VJ. (2020, December 15). *Is HR only a woman's profession?* Scikey Talent. https://www.scikey.ai/read-blog/133_is-hr-only-a-woman-s-profession.html

58. L'Oréal. (2023, October 25). *Chiffres-Clés.* https://www.loreal.com/fr/nos-engagements/pour-toutes-et-tous/promoting-diversity-and-inclusion/key-figures/

59. World Health Organization. (2021, March 9). *Devastatingly pervasive: 1 in 3 women globally experience violence*. https://www.who.int/news/item/09-03-2021-devastatingly-pervasive-1-in-3-women-globally-experience-violence

60. L'Oréal. (2021, April 2). *L'Oréal Paris family stands up against street harassment*. https://www.loreal.com/en/news/brands/loreal-paris-stand-up/

61. Accenture. (2022). *Working to accelerate equality for all*. https://www.accenture.com/fr-fr/about/inclusion-diversity/gender-equality

62. Sejournet, C. (2021, February 25). *La Consommation, un acte citoyen*. FemininBio. https://www.femininbio.com/societe/conseils-et-astuces/la-consommation-un-acte-citoyen-56043

63. Tan, S. (2024, May 7). *Unraveling brand boycotts: What are the top triggers for consumer boycotts across global markets?*. YouGov. https://business.yougov.com/content/49332-unraveling-brand-boycotts-what-are-top-triggers-for-consumer-boycotts-across-global-markets

64. Cormack, L., & Hatch, P. (2016, September 1). *ACCC takes Volkswagen to court over diesel emission claims*. The Sydney Morning Herald. https://www.smh.com.au/business/consumer-affairs/accc-takes-volkswagen-to-court-over-diesel-emission-claims-20160901-gr61ud.html

65. Forliance. (2023, March 7). *Why investing in sustainability is a smart business move* . https://forliance.com/news/2023/03/07/why-investing-in-sustainability-is-a-smart-business-move#:~:text=In%20fact%2C%20a%20study%20by%20Nielsen%20found%20that%2066%25%20of,positive%20social%20and%20environmental%20impact.

66. Segal, M. (2024, March 20). *Court rules KLM's sustainability-related advertising was misleading*. ESG Today. https://www.esgtoday.com/court-rules-klms-sustainability-related-advertising-was-misleading/

67. Dove. (2024). *The selfie talk: Self-esteem in the social media age*. https://www.dove.com/us/en/stories/campaigns/theselfietalk.html

68. Vestiaire Collective. (2023). 2023 Vestiaire Collective Impact Report. https://fashion-sustainability-report.vestiairecollective.com/media/site/eddac7b178-1687355851/23-vc-023.pdf

69. European Investment Bank. (2021). *The Ocean Plastics Reduction Guide*. European Investment Bank. https://www.eib.org/attachments/strategies/the_ocean_plastics_reduction_guide_en.pdf

70. European Parliament. (2018, October 12). *Plastic in the ocean: The facts, effects and new EU rules*. https://www.europarl.europa.eu/topics/en/article/20181005STO15110/plastic-in-the-ocean-the-facts-effects-and-new-eu-rules#:~:text=Plastic%20waste%20is%20increasingly%20polluting,in%20the%20EU%20by%202050

71. Horsman, S. (2024, March 22). *France becomes world's first country to legislate limits on Fast Fashion*. Monaco Life. https://monacolife.net/france-becomes-worlds-first-country-to-legislate-limits-on-fast-fashion/#:~:text=In%20mid%20March%2C%20France%20became,the%20Ecological%20Transition%2C%20Christophe%20B%C3%A9chu

72. *Innovation, science and technology*. (s. d.). Nestlé Global. https://www.nestle.com/about/research-development

73. Decathlon. (2023). *2023 Non-Financial Reporting Declaration*. https://www.decathlon-united.media/shared/pressfiles/modules/fichiers/decathlon_nfrd2023.pdf

74. *Institutional investors believe ESG factors are more important than financial metrics when evaluating a company's long-term attractiveness | Federated Hermes Limited*.

(s. d.). UK | Intermediary. https://www.hermes-investment.com/uk/en/intermediary/press/responsible-capitalism-survey/

75. *Re-evaluated performance of 100 most sustainable companies per Barron's in line with S&P 500*. (n.d.). Sustainable Invest. https://sustainableinvest.com/re-evaluated-performance-of-100-most-sustainable-companies-per-barrons-in-line-with-sp-500/

76. George, S. (2024, August 22). *Blackrock's support for ESG resolutions plummets.* Edie. https://www.edie.net/blackrocks-support-for-esg-resolutions-plummets/#:~:text=BlackRock%20confirmed%20that%2C%20in%20the,This%20is%20equivalent%20to%204%25

77. Allianz SE. (2023, August 4). *Global boiling : Heatwave may have cost 0.6pp of GDP*. https://www.allianz.com/en/economic_research/insights/publications/specials_fmo/global-heatwave-implications.html

78. Richardson, K. et al. (2023, September 13). *Earth beyond six of nine planetary boundaries*. Science Advances 9, 32. DOI: 10.1126/sciadv.adh2458.

79. Plc, U. (2024, April 18). *Unilever Climate & Nature Fund*. Unilever. https://www.unilever.com/sustainability/nature/unilever-climate-nature-fund/

80. Unilever. (n.d.). *Sustainable and regenerative sourcing*. https://www.unilever.com/sustainability/nature/sustainable-and-regenerative-sourcing/

81. Kering. (2020, October 14). The Fashion Pact : first steps towards industry transformation. https://www.kering.com/en/news/the-fashion-pact-first-steps-towards-industry-transformation/

82. Schenker, J.L. (2021). *Future4Care: Four Corporates Team To Make Europe A Global Leader in E-Health*. The Innovator. https://theinnovator.news/future4care-four-corporates-team-to-make-europe-a-global-leader-in-e-health/

83. B Lab UK. (2024, April 15). *UK B Corp community reaches 2,000*. https://bcorporation.uk/news-stories-and-events/news/uk-b-corp-community-reaches-2-000/

84. IPCC. (2022, April 4). *The evidence is clear: the time for action is now. We can halve emissions by 2030*. https://www.ipcc.ch/2022/04/04/ipcc-ar6-wgiii-pressrelease/

REFERENCES:

Alvarez, A. (2016, October 16). [Woman standing outdoor surrounded by bobbles during daytime]. Unsplash. https://unsplash.com/photos/woman-standing-outdoor-surrounded-by-bobbles-during-daytime-63YVMrL2d6g

Andre (n.d.). *Three trail runners, two men and a woman, running up a steep trail in the mountains in the Alps on a hot, bright summer day* [Photograph]. Adobe Stock. https://stock.adobe.com/images/three-trail-runners-two-men-and-a-woman-running-up-a-steep-trail-in-the-mountains-in-the-alps-on-a-hot-bright-summer-day/186488201?prev_url=detail

Choochaikupt, C. (2019, September 5). *Woman framing the sun with her hands in the sunrise, future concept of planning idea* [Photograph]. iStock Photo. https://www.istockphoto.com/fr/photo/la-femme-faisant-le-cadre-autour-du-soleil-avec-ses-mains-dans-le-lever-de-soleil-gm1171244365-324413153

Dmitrydesigner. (n.d.). *Women's rowing team on blue water* [Photograph]. Adobe Stock. https://stock.adobe.com/fr/images/women-s-rowing-team-on-blue-water/188302024?prev_url=detail

Dooley, I. (2017, October 10). *All Rise* [Photograph]. Unsplash. https://unsplash.com/photos/assorted-hot-air-balloons-flying-at-high-altitude-during-daytime-hpTH5b6mo2s

Filadrendo. (2017, December 10). *Human resources* [Photograph]. iStock Photo. https://www.istockphoto.com/fr/photo/les-ressources-humaines-gm889095186-246545963

G-Stockstudio. (2019, December 3). *Colleagues discussing new business* [Photograph]. https://www.istockphoto.com/fr/photo/collègues-discutant-de-nouvelles-affaires-gm1190157979-337268666

Hintze, H. (2018, April 6). *Great Sand Dunes National Park and Preserve, United States* [Photograph]. Unsplash. https://unsplash.com/photos/woman-standing-on-right-foot-and-raising-hands-at-the-bottom-of-sand-dunes-during-daytime-4ydjTMLKdR4

Itla. (2020, June 18). *Peaceful Protestors* [Photograph]. Stocksy. https://www.stocksy.com/photo/3247367/peaceful-protestors?vs=1

Khoury, A. (2019, October 2). [Boy on ladder under blue sky]. Unsplash. https://unsplash.com/photos/boy-on-ladder-under-blue-sky-Ba6llmAzl-k

Lopes, H. (2017, November 25). *Saturday. Summer. Beautiful sunny day, so my friends and I decided to make a picnic and watch the sundown. Pretty fun and relaxed day.* [Photograph]. Unsplash. https://unsplash.com/photos/four-person-hands-wrap-around-shoulders-while-looking-at-sunset-PGnqT0rXWLs

Miniseries. (2022, July 13). *Group of anonymous people raising their hands at a seminar* [Photograph]. iStock Photo. https://www.istockphoto.com/fr/photo/groupe-de-personnes-anonymes-levant-la-main-lors-dun-séminaire-gm1408304009-459207630

NEOM. (2023, April 28). *Amongst expansive red sands and spectacular sandstone rock formations, Hisma Desert – NEOM, Saudi Arabia | The NEOM Nature Reserve region is being designed to deliver protection and restoration of biodiversity across 95% of NEOM* [Photograph]. Unsplash. https://unsplash.com/photos/a-man-climbing-up-the-side-of-a-mountain-85ey1vFlwkc

Nowitz, R.T. (2016, July 25). *Hands of Children Playing Game* [Photography]. Getty Images. https://www.gettyimages.ae/detail/photo/hands-of-children-playing-game-royalty-free-image/583680440?searchscope=image%2Cfilm&adppopup=true

Sun, D. (2024, April 21). *A tree surrounded by a circular staircase* (Green Hill) [Photograph]. Unsplash. https://unsplash.com/photos/a-tree-inside-of-a-circular-building-with-a-skylight-c5siVo9jt3U

Sungkapukdee, P. (2020, Fevrier 14). *Man fixation compass on blurred background* [Photograph]. iStock Photo. https://www.istockphoto.com/fr/photo/boussole-de-fixation-dhomme-sur-le-fond-brouillé-pour-le-mode-de-vie-dactivité-à-gm1202534035-345279998

ZoneCreative. (2009, September 9). *Beautiful blonde hair Dandelion flower outdoors for children* [Photograph]. iStock Photo. https://www.istockphoto.com/fr/photo/belle-blonde-cheveux-fleur-de-pissenlit-en-plein-air-pour-les-enfants-gm182178294-10467139

Made in the USA
Coppell, TX
28 February 2025

46515084R00114